BOOTSTRAP

YOGA-BASED STRESS-MANAGEMENT PROGRAM

"For the first time in seven years, I'm getting a full night's sleep."

> Duane F., Command Sergeant Major, U.S. Army,
> Operation Enduring Freedom

"In just thirty minutes a day, BOOTSTRAP has left me relaxed and revitalized."

> Mike M., Colonel, U.S. Air Force,
> Operation Iraqi Freedom

"I finally feel in control of my life."

> Patrick V., Private First Class, U.S. Army,
> Vietnam

"My family and friends noticed a difference in me in just a few days of practice!"

> Richard H., Staff Sergeant, U.S. Army,
> Operation Iraqi Freedom

"I'm amazed at how great I feel. BOOTSTRAP is definitely something I'm grateful for."

> Sylvia H., Sergeant, U.S. Army,
> Operation Iraqi Freedom

"BOOTSTRAP made me a better father."

> Joaquin M., Sergeant, U.S. Marine Corps,
> Operation Iraqi Freedom

"BOOTSTRAP works wonders! From the first lesson, I felt my ability to manage stress grow."

> Mark H., U.S. Army, Chief Warrant Officer,
> Operation Iraqi Freedom

"More effective than I could have imagined. Do it for yourself. Do it for the people you care about."

> Dan M., Sergeant, U.S. Army,
> Gulf War

WAGING
I N N E R
PEACE

HOW 5,000 VETERANS

USED THE ANCIENT SECRETS

OF YOGA AND MINDFULNESS

TO RECLAIM THEIR LIVES FROM STRESS

(and how you can too)

Eric Walrabenstein

Published by
Yoga Pura Global Wellness Press
15440 N. 7th St, Suite 1
Phoenix, Arizona 85022

ISBN: 978-0-9973420-0-0

Disclaimer: Waging Inner Peace and the BOOTSTRAP system it contains have been specifically designed to interrupt the cycle of chronic stress that can arise as a result of traumatic events or the pressures of daily life. The system has been created, tested, and distributed independently of the Departments of Defense and Veterans Affairs. No part of this book or other support materials is intended to imply the official approval or endorsement of the United States Government, its agencies, or armed forces.

Consult with your doctor before beginning this or any other fitness program. While every effort has been made to ensure the effectiveness of this program, its use is at your own risk. The advice and strategies contained herein may not be suitable for every situation. The creators, producers, performers, sponsors, publishers, and distributors do not assume any liability for any loss, damage, or injury in connection with any use of this program or the instructions or advice expressed herein. Respect your limits. If at any time you should experience pain or discomfort while participating in this program, stop and consult your physician.

With gratitude to the men, women, and families
of the United States military, past and present.

WAGING INNER PEACE

CONTENTS

INSIDE OUT

Waging Inner Peace is not so much a book about stress as it is a book about getting what you want. Not the perfect career, the ideal relationship, or the snazzy new car mind you, but the thing that really matters: a happy life.

In case you haven't been paying attention, being a human being, no matter what your station in life, is a messy and difficult business. Career pressures, family obligations, health challenges, and the general demand of navigating an ever-changing and, at times, uncooperative world, can drag our otherwise blessed and happy lives into struggle, worry, anxiety, or worse.

In a word, life can be stressful—and this stress can seem to stand squarely between us and the happiness we deserve. And this is true whether your stress comes from a traumatic event like an automobile accident or military combat or from the simple act of laboring under the daily weight of living on the planet. Indeed stress is the enemy of our happiness.

1

The trouble is that in our quest for the stress-free and happy lives we desire, we get it backward. We too often put our attention on controlling our external circumstances, while ignoring the possibility of creating a stress-free, buoyant, and joyful experience directly—from the inside out. It's an oversight that, while at first may seem rather harmless, can leave great spans of our lives spent in unnecessary struggle and toil.

The truth is that we all have the capacity to synthesize greater wellness and ease in our lives quite independent from our circumstances, whatever they may be. Though admittedly most of us haven't tapped this ability to any significant degree, the ancient sages from great wisdom traditions like yoga can help.

For millennia, millions of these mind-body technologists have spent their lives perfecting a wide range of techniques that, when applied skillfully, can help us all live happier, more peaceful lives. This wisdom is at the core of Waging Inner Peace.

What follows is an exploration of sorts: one that will help us become ever more intimate with the inner workings of our mental and emotional lives; and one that is specifically designed to leave us more empowered to manage our stress and positively affect our sense of well-being in every corner of our lives.

Central to our inquiry will be a single question:

"How can we banish stress and synthesize more ease, joy, and positivity in every moment of our lives—independent of our circumstances?"

What you're about to read is the story of how over 5,000 hard-charging veterans were able to do just that. Using a customized yoga program in the privacy of their own homes, legions of our returning warriors have been able to reclaim their happiness by gaining mastery over their inner worlds of thoughts, attitudes, and emotions—even in the midst devastating psychological wounds, moral injuries, and life-sapping stress conditions, including post-traumatic stress.

The life-changing program they used, which is included in the pages of this book, is called BOOTSTRAP. It's a seven-week process of investigation and experimentation that employs a customized blend of ancient mind-body wisdom together with modern wellness principles to rebalance the nervous system and nourish both body and mind.

Originally created to help our troops and veterans recover from devastating cases of chronic stress, BOOTSTRAP is a program that has wide-spread relevance for anyone wanting to live a more artful and happy life.

THE ENEMY WITHIN

Epidemic is not a word to be thrown around lightly, but it is indeed one well-suited to describing the problem of stress in our modern world.

It's a well-known fact that rampant stress conditions are ravaging the ranks of our veterans all across the country. In fact, the U.S. Department of Veterans Affairs estimates that of the 2.7 million service members who have deployed to Iraq and Afghanistan, up to 20% have full blown post-traumatic stress disorder. But what is less well known is how this stress epidemic is in no way limited to our military populations.

The U.S. Centers for Disease Control agree and estimate that up to 90% of primary care physician visits among all Americans are linked to stress-related illness. Yes, 90%.

This is not to say that we are all rushing off to the doctor complaining about stress, rather it points to one of the things that makes stress so insidious: the way it masquerades as a myriad of annoying, but seemingly innocuous symptoms. Persistent anxiety, insomnia, difficulty concentrating, mood swings, anger, and irritability, to name a few, are conveniently written off by most of us as one of the many inevitable costs of living on the planet, when the truth is these pernicious conditions are all too often rooted in untreated stress.

As a result of this unfortunate misstep, most of us do very little to actively manage the stress in our lives and thereby allow the imbalanced nervous system to run unchecked. This wreaks havoc with a wide array of physiological functions, all of which makes us dangerously susceptible to a range of diseases from high blood pressure to heart disease, and depression to autoimmune conditions, and more. And this is to say nothing of the secondary effects stress has on our productivity, our relationships, and our happiness.

* * *

For those of us who do seek to take charge of our stress, an entirely different problem lies in wait. The fact is, that when it comes to restoring balance and ease to the body-mind, most of us are not only ill equipped, but are actually fighting the wrong battle.

The problem is created by the popular belief that stress comes primarily from our circumstances, that is to say, from the outside in. Our stressful job, our stressful relationship, our stressful living arrangements, and other factors in our external environment, the thinking goes, are what keep us mired in the cycle of stress and its crippling symptoms. But things aren't quite that simple.

In order for anything in our external environment to *seem* stressful, certain mechanisms in our internal world (specifically in the nervous system) must be triggered into action. For without the participation of these internal mechanisms, the stress response simply doesn't go. Have you ever asked yourself why sometimes a particular circumstance stresses you out, and at other times it barely bothers you at all? Well, now you know.

Making matters worse, these same internal mechanisms can be triggered even independent of a so-called stressful situation. This explains why you can find yourself basking comfortably on a beach in the Mexican Riviera while stressed out of your mind about what might be happening at work 4,000 miles away.

What all of this means is that our stress is acutely dependent on the happenings *inside* us, in our minds and nervous systems— and our efforts to manage it by manipulating our external world can only do so much. While it may seem to be a phenomenon that is foisted upon us from the outside in, stress, and its attendant mental and emotional turmoil, is to a very large degree an inside job.

* * *

Our confusion stems from something social psychologists refer to as *Fundamental Attribution Error.* The term refers to a phenomenon in which we assume the cause of an event to be one thing, when in fact, it is caused by a second, unacknowledged source.

The classic example is how we might conclude that a man running a stoplight is an irresponsible and hazardous driver, when in fact, he may be rushing to the hospital where his son was just admitted after a near fatal accident. In such a situation, many of us would likely attribute the man's behavior (running a stoplight) to one cause (irresponsibility) when it actually was caused by another, unconsidered cause (his son in the hospital).

The real problem with *Fundamental Attribution Error* is that it tends to put us to work solving the wrong problem. Rather than the stern talking-to we'd like to give the stoplight running man, what he really needs is a police escort to get to his son.

And so it goes with stress.

Like the overweight grocery clerk convinced that Twinkies are making him fat, too many of us remain focused on our external circumstances as the culprits behind our stress. It's not the Twinkies, it's what the clerk is doing with them (stuffing them down his gullet); and it's not our circumstances, it too is what we're doing with them (on the inside) that is causing our stress.

Instead of addressing the internal sources of stress head on, *Fundamental Attribution Error* has us spending our energies doggedly battling external stress triggers like our careers, our relationships, our finances, our families, and even our own personal histories. This leaves the real culprits behind the creation of our stress fully intact.

MANAGING YOUR HUMANNESS

While perhaps not at first evident, the fact that stress is largely created within us is good news indeed. For if stress was caused solely by our external circumstances, to experience the peace and happiness we crave, we would have to get everything around us to cooperate with our personal preferences.

Imagine having to struggle with everyone around you, to wrestle with every circumstance, just to be able feel relaxed and happy. What if you had to win the promotion and lose the weight; avoid the traffic and chide the rude clerk; acquire the right possessions and earn the right accolades, all just to feel okay?

Stress Fact:

The BOOTSTRAP system has been proven effective in reducing chronic stress in less than one hour per day.

If you're like most of us, it's not at all hard to imagine, because that's precisely how you spend a good chunk of your life. Even so, if a happy and relaxed life is what you're after, there's a decidedly more efficient way to go about it. It's a way that is actually made possible by the fact that stress is created within us.

Indeed, it is only due to stress' internal origins (albeit triggered at times by external events) that a life relatively free of its clutches is possible at all. And this is true no matter what our circumstances may be. Envision:

- Feeling calm, relaxed, and at the peak of happiness and efficiency despite life's challenges.

- Remaining comfortably at ease, right in the middle of the same situations that once sent you into a tailspin.

- Transforming the challenges and disappointments in life into blessings that bring even more peace and joy to your world.

This is the possibility that is unleashed when we turn our attention away from blaming our external circumstances for our stress and truly take charge of our internal world of thoughts, moods, and emotions directly. It's a skill that I call managing our humanness.

* * *

Managing our humanness invites us to consider the prospect of synthesizing the inner peace and happiness we so crave— from the inside out. Instead of having to rely upon the outside world of activities, accomplishments, and acquisitions to lift our spirits, we take control of the largely unexamined internal chain of events that can create and perpetuate negative thoughts, difficult emotions, and yes, the chronic stress response itself.

It's important to understand that the experience of stress is not the problem as much as it is the symptom of an underlying process. The stress response, which is natural and necessary for our survival by the way, involves a fairly predictable series of neuro-biochemical responses that can be understood and to a very large degree managed. Unfortunately, most of us remain relatively uninformed about what goes on under the hood of these body-minds we're trapped in, and thus, remain at the mercy of these physiological reactions.

With just a little effort however, we can become attuned to the mechanics of our inner world, including the mental habits that can help or hinder our well-being, and become well positioned to bring ourselves back toward a more harmonious balance no matter what our circumstances. But the first step is to stop blaming the world around us and seek to understand the true source of our stress and inner disturbance: the source within.

* * *

In the pages that follow, you'll find the complete story of BOOTSTRAP. From the epidemic that spurred its creation to the principles that informed the architecture of its ancient mind-body wisdom, you'll learn how to wield the power of mindfulness and yoga's lesser-known science of mind to restore balance to both body and mind. In the second half of the book, you'll get the opportunity put the actual seven-week BOOTSTRAP system to work in your own life—the exact same program that is right now helping thousands of our troops and veterans all around the world.

Step by step you'll be led through a one-of-a-kind approach that moves beyond mere relaxation techniques to involve you in a deliberate and measured exploration of the hidden mechanics through which stress can be perpetuated.

Remember while it's true that BOOTSTRAP was originally created to address military-related stress conditions, at its heart, the system is about helping you to manage your inner world of mind and emotions to increase joy and wellness in your daily life.

This means that even though we will be using stress as the subject of most of our conversations, and a healthy dose of military anecdotes in the actual program, please remember that the wisdom and techniques that follow are as relevant to you as to anyone walking about in one of these human body-minds.

We all have a great ability to synthesize an inner calm and happiness, despite our external circumstances, and it is my earnest hope that what follows will enable you to begin to elevate your own sense of peace and joy in every area of your life. And this is true whether you're experiencing the effects of chronic stress derived from a calamitous event, the persistent pressures of the ever-quickening pace of modern life, or you simply want to learn how to use ancient wisdom to live more joyously.

* * *

A final note, while the characters in the pages that follow are based on real people and events, names and details have been altered to honor the privacy of all—with the exception of your humble author, of course. Now, let's get to it.

CALL TO DUTY

It was late March 2006 when I got the call.

Bonnie Strauss was phoning. A long-time yoga student of mine, and a yoga teacher in her own right, Bonnie lived in Northbrook, Illinois, a stone's throw north of Chicago. Her son, Stephen, a U.S. Marine, had just returned from Iraq.

Bonnie and I had known each other for several years, in fact she had studied with me on a few different occasions, most notably during a retreat I led on yoga therapeutics in Florida. As soon as I picked up the phone, I could hear all was not well. Normally calm and measured by nature, Bonnie had a kind of warble to her voice that betrayed her distress.

"Hey E, I have a little issue I was hoping you might be able to help me with." She began, with the understatement of the year.

For fifteen minutes, Bonnie poured out Stephen's story.

The youngest of three children, with a brother in medical school and a sister in the Air Force, Stephen, like so many of us, had been particularly moved by the events of 9/11. Though at the time still too young to do anything about it, that all changed when a year later he graduated from high school and made a bee-line for the U.S. Marine Corps recruiting office.

Since his first day at boot camp at the Marine Corps Recruit Depot in San Diego, Stephen took to the Corps in a remarkable way. Despite the challenges, discomfort, and extreme discipline, Stephen flourished. For Stephen, the Marine Corps had provided a level of meaning and purpose to his life he had never felt before. As a Marine infantryman, he had an important role, people depended on him, and for the first time in his young life, he felt like what he did truly mattered. Stephen had, it seemed, found his place in the world.

* * *

Much to Bonnie's surprise, Stephen seemed to continue to thrive even into his deployment to Iraq.

That is, until he didn't. Everything changed in Fallujah.

Specifically it was during the second battle for the city that the full weight of the war came crashing down upon him. It was there that Stephen had been at the center of some of the fiercest battles the U.S. had seen—some say since Vietnam—and it was where he would be evacuated for wounds suffered in a bomb blast. But even more damaging, we were to later learn, was the loss of his best friend Matt to a sniper's bullet in the earliest days of the fighting.

Fortunately, Stephen's wounds were minor and he was soon returned to duty. He finished out his deployment, but without the same zeal he once had, and then returned to his stateside home in Camp Pendleton on the coast just north of San Diego. It was there that things took a significant turn for the worse.

Nearly as soon as the homecoming parties were over, Stephen's mood began to change. Jennifer, Stephen's fiancée, confided to Bonnie in a series of late-night phone calls that his usual happy-go-lucky personality had been replaced by something much darker. Vacillating between bouts of isolating depression and explosive outbursts of anger, Stephen's difficulty regulating his emotions was becoming a very real concern.

It was shortly thereafter that the official diagnosis came. As everyone had begun to suspect, Stephen had a rather well-developed case of post-traumatic stress.

* * *

Post-traumatic stress (PTS), also known as post-traumatic stress disorder, is a condition that arises as a result of experiencing a highly-stressful or terrifying event. In overly simplistic terms, the nervous system has been knocked out of balance causing a whole range of potentially debilitating symptoms like insomnia, night terrors, outbursts of anger, difficulty concentrating, and others.

While the devastating effects of PTS are inarguable, the irony lives in the fact that it derives from the nervous system performing largely as designed. Whenever faced with circumstances that may be injurious to one's wellbeing, the autonomic nervous system is supposed to switch into its sympathetic, or fight-or-flight mode (sometimes called fight-flight-freeze), enervating a range of physiological functions designed to ready you to cope with the danger at hand: increasing heart rate, tensing muscles, heightening attention, and pouring an entire range of stress hormones into the system to name a few. This is precisely what is happening with PTS.

The problem arises when this appropriate response to danger becomes triggered by inappropriate situations, that is, situations in which no real danger exists. The nervous system has learned that a loud bang is a bullet flying toward your head; so when the neighbor's car backfires you find yourself face down on the floor of your breakfast nook faster than you can say Count Chocula.

In chronic stress conditions, the over stimulation of this life-preserving process results in the fight-or-flight response becoming the nervous system's dominant mode of operation (something called sympathetic dominance in the parlance of neuroscience). This spawns the crippling symptoms mentioned above.

Yes, post-traumatic stress is not a disease; it is a normal reaction to an abnormal situation.

Even more problematic however, the primary symptoms of PTS can, and often do, lead to a range of catastrophic social problems: disintegrating families, ruined careers, substance abuse, and suicide are just few the issues that commonly befall chronic stress sufferers. What's more, recent studies have shown that the effects of PTS can be transmitted to our children and other family members as well, something referred to secondary PTS.

So, chronic stress, whether diagnosed as PTS or something less, is nothing to be trifled with. Its effects are far more dangerous than we might think and, if not treated properly, can wreak havoc with all that we hold precious—for a lifetime.

* * *

After he was officially diagnosed with PTS, Stephen was placed on a treatment regimen including various talk therapies and a dizzying array of medications: Prozac for mood, Ambien for sleep, clonazepam for anxiety, and clonidine, a high blood pressure drug that in Stephen's case was prescribed for nightmares. While the medications did have some effect in calming his symptoms, they also carried a litany of nasty side-effects that in many ways were worse than the stress symptoms themselves.

Making matters worse, as Stephen was fully aware, the diagnosis of post-traumatic stress could mean disaster for his career in the Marine Corps. Despite the best efforts of the Corps, as well as the leadership of the Department of Defense, significant stigma about the condition and the associated mental health services designed to treat it remained strong. The possibility of damaging, or worse, losing the career that had brought so much purpose to his life was itself a source of near-constant anxiety.

Sadly, notwithstanding the efforts to bring his stress under control, in the end, Stephen was medically separated from the Marine Corps for his service-connected post-traumatic stress. He had reluctantly joined the ranks of the hundreds of thousands of veterans struggling with disabilities linked to their service and had since moved home to Chicago.

After laying out Stephen's story, Bonnie asked "So E, do you think you can help?"

I paused. The short answer was yes, I was pretty sure I could. I had been helping people heal from post-traumatic stress and other chronic stress conditions for many years. And better, of my hundreds of clients, a great many had struggled with PTS derived from military experiences. So Stephen's problems were definitely in my wheel house.

* * *

At the time, the war in Iraq was at a fevered pitch with deployments to Afghanistan picking up at an accelerating rate. As more and more of our service members were rotated through multiple deployments to the war zones, the United States Departments of Defense and Veterans Affairs were beginning to realize they had a full-blown epidemic on their hands.

Things were bad it seemed and were getting worse. Not only were thousands returning from the battlefield with catastrophic physical wounds, it was becoming obvious that this was but a fraction of a larger problem. Hundreds of thousands were arriving home with invisible psychological wounds that could be every bit as debilitating. On top of that, these types of mental and emotional injuries often lingered untreated for months or years before being diagnosed—and treatment was as time-consuming as it was difficult.

The fact that service members and veterans were appearing for help at the door of my center in Phoenix was evidence of the system's overwhelm.

As a former U.S. Army infantry officer, the problem was more personal for me than for many, and it's why we threw open our doors to service members and veterans with an entire range of free classes and workshops.

Although the regularly-scheduled yoga and meditation classes were helping, it quickly became clear that a more intentional intervention was called for. Not only was an approach that more comprehensively addressed the inner causes of chronic stress required, but with hundreds of thousands struggling with PTS, it was obvious that we wouldn't be able to make even the smallest dent using only the 6,000 square feet of my Arizona center. We needed a process that could be scaled to help thousands around the world.

* * *

I first fell in love with yoga back in 1992, or at least I thought I did. In the time since, I've come to realize that my love affair wasn't with yoga at all. I was simply confused. More on that in a bit.

As confusions go however, I'll be the first to admit this was a pretty healthy one. For it was my confusion that led me to dive headlong into the practice of yoga, to dedicate myself to the study of its ancient source documents, to experiment with its myriad tools and concepts, and to complete multiple yoga teacher training programs.

In the years that followed, I would found one of the largest yoga centers in Arizona, create the state's first master-level yoga teacher training program, develop one of the nation's first professional-level yoga nidra certification courses, and of course develop the BOOTSTRAP Yoga System which is right now at work repairing the lives of thousands of our troops and veterans all around the world.

But as I said, I didn't really fall in love with yoga.

What I loved was not a 5,000 year old science born in a land on the other side of the globe. Nor was it the practice of moving my body into and out of a series of challenging postures. It wasn't even the use of breath and focused attention to clear my mind and calm my emotions. No, yoga wasn't what I was in love with: It was clarity. It was vitality. It was wellness. Yoga was simply the means that allowed me to get there.

The fact is yoga is merely a set of tools, like the paint brushes of the painter, or the hammer and chisel of the sculptor, that had helped me to create a day-to-day experience of joy and lightness in my life I hadn't known for years. I was charmed by the feeling of ease, enamored with the experience of happiness, and captivated by the healthy and joyous relationship I had fallen into with my body, mind—and the world.

I realize that this may seem like a trivial point, yet I want to be clear: My work, including this book and the BOOTSTRAP system that it contains, is not about yoga—it is about you and your life at its best and happiest.

And while it's true that my work does draw much from yoga's ancient science of mind (together with a collection of other traditions), at its heart, it is about helping you to awaken and cultivate the balanced, easeful condition that is in fact your natural state.

* * *

For years before Bonnie's call, the methodology I had been using with clients with stress injuries was focused on customizing yoga posture sequences, breath exercises, and mindfulness practices to calm the nervous system. This strategy was, and to a very large extent still is, the de facto methodology most yoga and mindfulness-based stress-management programs employ. And, to be fair, it's a valid strategy too.

Yoga postures, rightly performed, can have a profound and immediate effect on the nervous system—and an out-of-control stress response. I say "rightly performed", because how you perform a given posture is as important as the yoga posture itself.

The truth is that a yoga posture can be performed in a way that moves the out-of-control nervous system toward greater balance and relaxation; and the *very same* posture can also be performed in a way that can actually worsen the stress response— and perpetuate imbalance. The secret is in understanding the nuances involved in the application of the technique; something that we will discuss later in the book.

But as much progress as I was seeing in my clients using this approach, I soon began to notice a rather troubling phenomenon. Time and again I would watch as a yoga session would yield a deep and rejuvenating effect, and yet soon thereafter, a significant percentage of every group would rebound right back to their previously stressed and anxious states. Often in just minutes.

Now, just so we're clear, this is not to say that this traditional approach didn't create steady and incremental progress toward more balance and ease in the nervous system. For the truth is, it did—and impressively so.

It's just that there seemed to be an awful lot of backsliding; backsliding that I strongly believed might be otherwise avoided if only I could devise the right strategy.

* * *

I'll admit, my effort to create a yoga-based process for use as a treatment modality for post-traumatic stress was not without its detractors.

Whenever I touted the healing potential of yoga, especially to people who really understand post-traumatic stress (and I do mean *really* understand, like researchers and psychologists who have devoted entire careers to the study and treatment of the condition), more often than not, I get a doubting, sideward glance or worse, a semi-exasperated roll of the eyes dismissing me as yet another patchouli-soaked, granola-infused nut case who's somehow slipped outside the wire of the yoga farm.

But it's not their fault.

You see, their doubt and even downright incredulity is rightly placed. It stems from the fact that post-traumatic stress is a dizzying, complex condition that can require a sophisticated array of interdictory strategies to even begin to bring it under control.

And one other thing.

What passes for yoga in today's culture (and thus what is accepted to be yoga by the vast majority of Americans) is but a shadow of the full and authentic practice. Let's face it, if your entire experience of yoga has been one of performing a series of postures in mindful synchronization with breath and a grooving playlist, well, let's just say that your misgivings are well placed.

You see, as yoga has migrated west, it has changed. Or more accurately, a redacted form of yoga has evolved. Little by little, one of the most powerful and comprehensive psycho-physical healing modalities the world has ever seen has become a mere caricature of its true self.

What's not commonly known is that yoga is an ancient science of mind (and yes, I said science and mind). When at its best, this robust and powerful system employs both somatic (body-focused) and cognitive (mind-focused) techniques that can restore balance to the out-of-control processes that fuel a great many sources of our physical, mental, and emotional distress—including post-traumatic stress. Perhaps most importantly for our purposes here, the practice has almost nothing to do with touching your toes, balancing on one foot, or standing about in funny-shaped postures.

* * *

From the perspective of healing chronic stress conditions, it is the effectiveness of this physically-oriented version of yoga that is, in some ways, its greatest downfall.

Because it is so useful in calming the nervous system through somatic means, too many of its teachers are led to ignore the lesser-known cognitive aspects of the practice that can create such powerful and lasting healing.

I speak from experience as this is precisely how my training let me down.

The truth is that the bulk of yoga teachers are indeed well trained in yoga's body-oriented techniques, but the practice's rich history of cognitive investigation, behavioral experimentation, and introspective evaluation are very rarely taught (or learned). For your Saturday morning yoga-based exercise class, this is not such a big deal; however, for healing complex conditions like chronic stress, it leaves us with a woefully incomplete solution.

That's because the inclusion of both the cognitive and the somatic aspects of the tradition makes for an especially potent formula, especially for those with post-traumatic stress and other stress conditions. When we employ both of these elements simultaneously, it allows for healing that, in a manner of speaking, moves from both ends towards the middle.

On the one hand, we have the somatic aspects of the practice working directly to calm the nervous system and interrupt the out-of-control stress response that is a hallmark of such conditions.

Simultaneously on the other hand, cognitive investigations reveal the often hidden mental tendencies that fuel the perpetuation of the chronically over-activated stress response. The recognition of such tendencies sets the stage for them to be released, or at the very least reduced, and enables the nervous system to maintain its natural relaxed state, untriggered by unnecessary internal conflict.

* * *

It became clear that the backsliding that so many of my clients were experiencing—even after a deeply rejuvenating relaxation practice—was being caused by a rush of negative memories and harmful patterns of thinking that would draw them right back into the stress spiral. It was something that called for a remedy more comprehensive than mere physical movement and mindfulness.

To put it another way, while the posture-oriented yoga practices were addressing the effects the imbalanced nervous system had *in the body*, they were doing little to uproot the deep-seated stress-producing tendencies *in the mind*.

It was this insight that spawned my earnest exploration of the aspects of yoga that had been largely left behind by modern culture: those aimed directly at the management of the mind like *pratyahara* or withdrawal from the senses; *dharana* or concentrated attention; and *vairagya* or non-attachment to name a few.

* * *

Back in October of 1980 as a scrawny, seventeen year old, I found myself in a dark and lonely parking garage in Sacramento, California. It was there that I was attacked.

There were about eight of them, much bigger than I was and

they wanted my wallet—and apparently some practice punching and kicking the crap out of a skinny kid from out of town.

They got what they wanted.

As attacks go, it wasn't particularly brutal. I had a knife held to my throat and was beaten pretty badly, but luckily wasn't stabbed or shot. I was left with my left eye crimson purple and swollen shut together with a collection of aches and bruises—and, of course, a nifty trip to the emergency room.

But as mild as it was physically, the attack had an effect on my nervous system.

For years, dark enclosed spaces sent me into a low-grade panic, and people who looked and dressed like my attackers stirred up a powerful sense of anxiety in me. For no reason at all (or so I thought), I would find myself racked with angst or fear or even anger—and as soon as it gripped me it seemed to spiral out of control.

It all left me wondering: "when things would get back to normal?" Unfortunately they didn't for nearly 15 years. Now I know why.

Without getting overly technical, a little-known region of my brain called the amygdala had "tagged" certain situations as dangerous:

- Enclosed spaces.
- Seemingly deserted areas.
- Dimly lit areas.
- Groups of people having a particular look.

These "tagged" situations became stress triggers for me, each one sending my nervous system into fight-or-flight overdrive anytime they were encountered.

While in western parlance, we would say that the event had been emotionally tagged, from the yogic perspective it is an example of a powerful *samskara* being formed.

* * *

Samskara is a Sanskrit word that translates loosely as impression, and refers to any one of the many tendencies of mind that are largely responsible for driving our behaviors and perceptions of the world. Maybe best thought of as one part belief and one part habit, *samskaras* work quietly behind the scenes affecting our every thought, action, and utterance.

Picture a uniformed police officer knocking on your door. What would that mean to you, and how would you likely react? The answer? It depends upon your *samskaras*.

- The spouse of a police officer might have her heart drop with dread.

- A drug dealer might experience fear and dash out the back door.

- A retired police chief might feel elated about being visited by a friend.

Each of these people, and in fact, each and every human being on the planet, has a different mix of *samskaras* based upon their experiences and upbringing. And thus, each and every one of us has our unique way of seeing and responding to our world.

- Some of us think pit bulls are cute and cuddly; others are wracked with fear in their presence.

- Some feel people to be good and trustworthy; others are suspicious of all they come in contact with.

- Some people are self-confident and motivated; others are hobbled by low self esteem and doubt.

These opinions, points of view, and interpretations are all things driven by a particular mix of *samskaras*, or mental tendencies. Perhaps best thought of as bits of programmed code in our brains, these impressions are not fixed nor are they predominantly inborn. They are learned as a result of the experiences we have as we roll through life. Everything you've ever heard, seen, tasted, or experienced in any way has impacted your nervous system and *samskaras*. Some greatly and some less so, but everything has an effect.

But here's the important part: because *samskaras* are learned, they also can be unlearned. It's a fact made possible by something called neuroplasticity, a term that refers to the malleable nature of our brains, and it paves the way for great transformation and healing. This was something I had learned in my own journey back to health and balance.

During my attack, my nervous system had *learned* that certain situations were dangerous—but the fact was that they weren't universally so. This is why I found myself triggered into stress episodes in places like stairwells and parking garages even when they were quite obviously safe.

It wasn't until my nervous system had *unlearned* this fact (or we could say that the unhelpful *samskaras* were neutralized), that I was free to move about my life without the constant stress events that tormented me.

Thirty-five years ago, lying bruised and bloodied on the cold concrete of a downtown parking garage, you could have never convinced me of the fortunate nature of the event, but it turns out that the incident and the stress condition it created would guide me in shaping the BOOTSTRAP system that would help thousands upon thousands.

* * *

As I began to write the BOOTSTRAP curriculum, I shared early drafts with friends from both the yoga and military communities. I wanted to make sure the instruction was as clear as possible, and of course make the program readily accessible to those in the armed forces. I am acutely aware that the yoga and military populations exist largely at opposite ends of the cultural spectrum and I needed to bridge that gap in a way that would make the program relatable for all.

Here I'd like to acknowledge a true debt of gratitude to so many who endured these late-night, caffeine-fueled discussions about the process, the manuscript, and the many challenges to making this program a reality. These conversations were instrumental in refining the tone and approach of the system, but perhaps more importantly, they helped me to see how important a portable, self-paced version of this work could be in helping a great many more people than just Bonnie and Stephen, who, as of this writing, is doing much, much better (he and Jennifer have married and he is currently pursuing a degree in applied psychology).

What you are about to read is the *unedited* BOOTSTRAP curriculum designed specifically for our troops and veterans. When preparing this book for distribution, I had a great many conversations with my team about whether we should alter the program for release to the general public. While we considered arguments on both sides, we ultimately decided to preserve the program in its original, proven form.

What that means is that in the pages that follow, you'll find many examples from military life, but please don't be put off. As we saw earlier, as far as the nervous system is concerned, the source of your stress is largely irrelevant, no matter if your stress came from combat in a military conflict or the combat of a 20-year high stress career. What's more, managing stress isn't about managing stress so much as it is about managing the underlying internal process that contribute to it. Again, it's about managing your humanness.

The truth is that every aspect of the program is completely relevant to anyone experiencing stress symptoms like insomnia, anxiety, depression, difficulty concentrating, or anger as well as those simply wishing to live more artfully and happily.

Lastly, for those yoga aficionados among us, you'll notice that

I've chosen not to use a lot of yoga terminology. As mentioned before, my intention was to craft a process that was effective and accessible to people from all walks of life—independent of whether they had an affinity for the practice of yoga.

However, for those curious about the program's yogic sources, I've included brief annotations at the beginning of each weekly lesson to help you understand how each relates to yoga's ancient wisdom.

* * *

A few final notes for those readers interested in engaging in the full process (recommended), not just reading about it:

- Read the following *Introduction to BOOTSTRAP* section prior to beginning the program.

- Move through the subsequent lessons at a pace of one lesson per week. For the system to work, it is imperative that you spend a week with each concept and set of techniques.

- Make sure you engage in the experiments and techniques fully, they are required elements of the healing process.

- Move forward with a calm objectivity, becoming overly serious, can backfire by causing additional stress.

Enjoy the ride.

BOOTSTRAP®

Yoga-Based Stress Management System

BOOTSTRAP®
Armed Forces Stress-management System

BOOTSTRAP is a seven-week process that employs a unique combination of physical and mental practices mined from modern science and the ancient and powerful wisdom of yoga and mindfulness. Far beyond a simple stretching or stress-relief workout, the process you are about to embark on effectively restores balance to all the systems of the body and mind while relieving the potentially crippling effects of stress. It is a system that understands the workings of human neurology and one that will calm your mind, increase your vitality, transform your relationships, and boost your enthusiasm for life.

To be clear, BOOTSTRAP is not a typical yoga program. It is a purpose designed stress-management system developed specifically to dismantle the processes through which military duty-related stress is created and perpetuated [author's note: as mentioned earlier, the BOOTSTRAP process is equally effective with stress from non-military sources as well]. While the program does borrow from the ancient wisdom of yoga, at its heart it is about you mastering the internal sources of stress and stepping into a life brimming with peace and possibility. It is a potent system that has, over the years, helped thousands of people to do just that.

BOOTSTRAP acknowledges that avoiding stressful situations is not a workable long-term solution. Let's face it—no matter how hard we try to control things, life can still be challenging, difficult, and at times even frightening. Because of this, the BOOTSTRAP approach has been designed to help you to meet and even embrace the challenges in your life with a renewed sense of ease.

Stress Fact:

BOOTSTRAP requires no prior experience of any kind.

The system works by enlisting the nervous system to interrupt the mental habits and unconscious tendencies that fuel the continuation of unwanted stress. Using a unique combination of learning and practical techniques that can be integrated into your everyday life, the program has been crafted to fit within your busy modern lifestyle. In less than one hour a day and with no previous experience of any kind, you'll be set on a course for relaxed, ease-filled living. Only one thing is required for your success: your commitment.

For this reason we ask that you take a moment to set an intention, one that will support you while you engage in the BOOTSTRAP process. We've created this program as a commitment to you and service members and veterans all over the world; we now ask that you commit, not to us but to yourself, your health, your happiness, and your greatest potential.

Take a moment now to solidify your commitment by completing the form below.

A Commitment to Your Best Life

I _____ *commit myself to*
    your name here

my own increased well-being, vitality, and productivity by

dedicating just one hour a day to the BOOTSTRAP practices

for the next seven weeks. I realize that there will be times

when other life priorities will seem to stand in the way of my

BOOTSTRAP practices, yet I commit to creating the time in

my life to fully participate in the process. I do this because

I recognize that the benefits to my health and well-being

derived from the BOOTSTRAP process will positively affect

not only myself but my loved ones and every other aspect of

my life as well.

_____

Your signature here   *Date*

Stress: Friend or Foe?

Stress is a part of life. That's a fact. It seeps into our homes, our schools, and our workplaces—and there's no one for whom that is more true than the devoted members of our armed forces.

The good news is that stress in the right doses can keep us alert, help us grow, and build our confidence. In fact, stress can have some surprisingly positive effects. In combat, for example, stress heightens our awareness, sharpens our senses, and increases our energy to meet the rigorous demands of the job at hand. In combat, stress can save your life.

But stress can also be a debilitating presence. No matter who you are, how strong you are, or how well you've been trained, stress can build to a point at which it begins to interfere with the natural functioning of mind and body. When the body's stress reaction becomes overloaded, we find ourselves stuck in a heightened state of awareness that depletes our physical energy, saps our mental agility, and can leave us suffering from a host of potentially crippling symptoms, including:

- Frequent headaches
- Chronic insomnia
- Recurring nightmares
- Difficulty concentrating
- Tightness of chest
- Disturbing flashbacks
- Difficulty breathing
- Recurring anxiety
- Irritability and mood swings
- Chronic fatigue

Making matters worse, when left unmanaged, the long-term effects of chronic stress can increase your susceptibility to a number of potentially life-threatening conditions, including depression, heart disease, obesity, diabetes, and more.

The term *stress*, as we think of it today, was coined by Hungarian-born endocrinologist Hans Selye in 1936. He defined the term as "the nonspecific response of the body to any demand for change." To put it in a slightly different way, stress is your body's attempt to respond to a particular circumstance in a way that will best ensure its survival.

What this means is that stress is a natural and necessary part of the normal functioning of the human organism. We don't want to completely rid ourselves of stress, but rather to manage it in a way that serves our needs while averting the harmful effects associated with the chronic overstressed state. The scientific experimentation and the objective observations integrated into the BOOTSTRAP process enable us to do just this.

Our experience of stress derives largely from the actions of the *sympathetic nervous system*, which is responsible for preparing the body and the mind to deal with threatening circumstances. When faced with a threat, real or perceived, the *sympathetic nervous system* releases stress hormones into the bloodstream (primarily epinephrine, norepinephrine, and cortisol) that prompt the body and the mind into a state of heightened readiness. It's a process commonly referred to as the *fight-or-flight response* (sometimes also *fight, flight, freeze response*) and it's one designed to enhance our chances of survival in a potentially perilous situation.

A few of the effects of the *fight-or-flight response* are:
- Increased heart rate and respiration
- Heightened awareness of surroundings
- Increased blood flow to skeletal muscles
- Decreased digestive function
- Inhibited sexual function

In short, the body is preparing itself do deal with the perceived threat. It does this by temporarily directing energy resources toward those functions that are required to fight or flee (like heart, lungs, and muscles) and away from those functions that are not immediately needed (like digestion and sexual function). It's a system that has served well us for thousands upon thousands of years, and is one that continues to serve us today—but with some limitations.

You see, for early man, nearly all threats, from a forest fire to a charging rhino, could be dealt with by way of one of two basic strategies: fighting your way through the danger or running away from it (hence the term *fight-or-flight*). But alas, in the modern world, much has changed, and this is at least partially responsible for the challenges we face with managing stress today. But more on that later.

The main takeaway here is that stress is indeed a positive and important component in the healthy functioning of the human organism. In high-stress situations such as combat, the body's stress response initially provides the energy and the focus for dealing optimally with whatever threats are present; stress helps to ensure our survival.

Stress Fact:

Stress is normal. In fact, it's a necessary part of the healthy functioning of the human organism. The trouble begins when stress accumulates without being released. This can occur as a result of life circumstances as well as through unconscious habits of both body and mind.

Where things go wrong however, is when the recuperative ability of the nervous system becomes overwhelmed by the severity of the stress response. This can happen as a result of the intensity of a single episode or because of the cumulative effect of a long series of stressful, but less intense, situations.

For most people, it makes sense that the intensity of a single life-threatening event, like an encounter with a roadside bomb or a violent car accident, can have such long-lasting effects on the nervous system. It's how the cumulative effects of lower grade stress can have such an effect—how, for instance, the daily stresses of career and family can end up so debilitating—that is a more perplexing question. For that reason I want to take a moment to visit how prolonged exposure to even seemingly manageable levels of stress can spiral out of control.

As you might imagine, the stress response evolved long, long ago to help us cope efficiently with the various threats we would face in the natural world. A tiger, a tornado, or a pterodactyl would all prompt the body into its highest state of readiness. Unlike today, the threats of old would typically pass in a relatively short period of time, allowing the body to relax back into its natural rhythm. Stressors in our modern world, however, more often than not occur over a protracted period of time. We've traded a twelve minute tiger encounter for a twelve month combat deployment, a twenty nine minute tornado watch for a twenty nine year high-stress career. And it's this change in duration that sets us up for potential difficulty.

The body responds to a prolonged stressor in the same way it would to a quick encounter with a natural predator, triggering the *fight-or-flight response*, releasing stress hormones into the body, and inducing the enhanced state of readiness needed to ensure survival. And while this response initially may be rather moderate, over time the demands placed on the body by the induced stress response exceed its endurance capacity and, as a result, the stress response itself can become an additional stressor. It's this vicious cycle that can cause our health and well-being to suffer dramatically.

Making matters worse, when faced with significant stressors, a couple of internal conditions can arrive on the scene. These circumstances, which we'll call *conditions of perpetuation*, can help to further derail the natural, healthy functioning of the nervous system and trap us in the cycle of chronic stress. They are:

FROZEN STRESS RESPONSE – As a result of overstimulation, the body can become trapped in a persistently-triggered *fight-or-flight response*, even in the total absence of any threat. The *stress response* has been frozen in the "on" position. This phenomenon creates the same drain on the resources of the body and the mind as does an actual prolonged threat, despite the fact that no danger exists. As a result of this habituated stress response, the nervous system is not allowed to return to its natural state of relaxation and is instead continually taxed by the overactive and inappropriate demands created by the *sympathetic nervous system.*

Frozen stress response is common in a wide range individuals who have been exposed to a prolonged threat like a combat deployment as well as for persons exposed to a single traumatic event.

MISPERCEPTION OF THREAT – Rather than suggesting that a threat triggers our *fight-or-flight response*, it would be more accurate to say that it is the *perception* of threat that kicks the *sympathetic nervous system* into action. In other words, we can be in the presence of a threat, not perceive it as such and remain unaffected; or we can *perceive* a threat that in reality is not a threat at all and be thrown for a loop. An old yogic story of a man petrified with fear after mistaking a coiled rope for a snake illustrates the principle quite well.

The story has a man stumbling upon a snake in the twilight. He's immediately overcome by fear—his *sympathetic nervous system* has kicked into high gear. Trembling, sweating, and literally paralyzed, his friend walks up behind him with a lantern, and in the glow of the light it's revealed that the "snake" is merely a coiled rope. Immediately, the man's fear subsides. This is classic *misperception of threat.*

While the misperception of a threat may not seem a likely occurrence, the truth is that for some of us, the effects of memory can trigger such misperceptions with striking regularity. Memories that mentally re-create threatening circumstances of the past again and again are common, both while sleeping and awake. What's more, because the mind associates like experiences, a seemingly harmless occurrence such as a car backfire can trigger the *fight-or-flight response* that was first initiated by gunfire that occurred long ago. This can happen unconsciously and without warning.

Thus it's not difficult to see how this kind of *misperception of threat* can lead to regular and unwarranted activation of the *stress response.*

Either of these internal conditions can combine with our already stressful circumstances and demand significantly more of the nervous system than it was designed handle. Imagine sending 1,000 volts through an electrical circuit designed for only 120 volts and you'll get the idea. When this happens, body's natural efforts to restore balance and ease are disturbed.

In normal functioning, the *sympathetic nervous system* is responsible for the initiation of the stress response, its partner, the *parasympathetic nervous system*, is responsible for bringing the body back to restorative relaxation. Sympathetic induces tension; parasympathetic induces relaxation. However, when external stressors combine with the *conditions of perpetuation*, the natural functioning of the parasympathetic system is inhibited and the sympathetic system becomes overworked. The balancing act between these two aspects of the nervous system is disturbed, and tensions build without being released.

This phenomenon is called *sympathetic dominance*, referring to the fact that the *fight-or-flight response* has become the nervous system's dominant mode of operation. It all adds up to a situation in which stress accumulates without allowing the body and the mind the time or means for recovery. Making matters worse, our efforts to relieve stress can combine with our existing mental habit patterns to further worsen the stress response. These *stress intensifiers* are explored in lessons two and three of the BOOTSTRAP system.

Fortunately, there is hope. Although our chronic stress can be exacerbated by the *conditions of perpetuation*, we are able to interrupt this dysfunction with a combination of understanding and cognitive and somatic techniques. This, of course, is what the BOOTSTRAP process is designed to do.

One final note: Although the BOOTSTRAP system can be employed as a stand-alone stress-management solution, the program recognizes the effectiveness of other complementary stress-relief services and seeks not to replace but rather to augment other treatments or programs you may be participating in.

This self-managed program is designed to be a portable system that can be performed whether you are at home or deployed. Its simple yet powerful tools will put you back in control of your life, leaving you rejuvenated and reinvigorated and with a new level of focus and drive to complete your mission—both on duty and at home.

The BOOTSTRAP® Process

The BOOTSTRAP process is about mastering your stress, not simply escaping it. It's about confronting the underlying mental tendencies that breathe life into the continued cycle of anxiety and struggle. It's about empowering you to restore a natural and healthful vitality to the body and mind simply, safely, and efficiently.

To do this, you'll be asked to serve as a kind of scientist. From here on, think of yourself as a *"stressologist."* Throughout the BOOTSTRAP process, you'll be assigned various experiments to perform, both in your home (think of it as your Stress Lab)

Stress Fact:

Stress-management differs from stress-relief. Stress-relief programs seek to reduce or eliminate stress currently being experienced; stress-management efforts go a step further. Not only does the stress-management approach reduce stress, it empowers users to manage future stressful situations skillfully and with ease.

BOOTSTRAP is a stress-management program.

and in your daily life, with the goal of learning as much as you can about the hidden workings of stress in your life. Through your careful study and meticulous experimentation, you will be able to use BOOTSTRAP's unique three-pronged approach to neutralize the unconscious mental tendencies that create unnecessary stress and anxiety.

Stress Fact:

BOOTSTRAP is designed to help you understand how unwanted stress is created and to empower you to manage it effectively throughout your life.

It is important to note that these harmful mental tendencies are in no way unique to military veterans or other survivors of trauma. We all have these tendencies to some degree; it's just that the consequences of these habits of mind are drastically more damaging for those who have been exposed to intense trauma in their lives. Said another way, the stress that military service can cause is a normal human response to trauma. You are not flawed.

The three-pronged BOOTSTRAP approach is:
1. RECOGNIZE
2. RELEASE
3. RESTORE

RECOGNIZE: Working in your home-based Stress Lab as well as in your daily life, you will examine how your actions, your thinking, and your relationship to an experience affect your stress level and well-being. The first step is to become aware of your unconscious mental habits and to connect the dots between these habits and their effects in your life. Here you will experience a scientific fact: the way you *relate* to a situation has as much effect on your experience as does the situation itself.

RELEASE: Once you are aware of your self-sabotaging mental tendencies, the ones that fuel your chronic stress, you are able to begin deliberately releasing them. When you're freed from your unintentional participation in the internal habits that further stress, the cycle that perpetuates chronic stress can be lessened.

RESTORE: The body and the mind seek health and well-being. Your body wants to be at ease, it craves healthy balance, and, best of all, it has the ability to create this—if only we can remove the obstacles that keep us stuck in the vicious cycle of chronic stress. The first two steps of the BOOTSTRAP process are designed to do just this. This allows the body and mind to get on with the business of healing and allow the neurological system to return to its normal balanced state.

The first two steps of our process, *recognize* and *release*, remove the obstacles. This allows the nervous system to be *restored* while we further support the process by giving the body what it needs in terms of rest, nutrition, and care. We will employ these three steps in each of our weekly lessons.

The BOOTSTRAP® Techniques

We've seen what the BOOTSTRAP process is designed to do—now it's time to look at the specific techniques that you, as a *stressologist*, will use to achieve your objectives.

Each week for the next seven weeks, you will review a new lesson that explores how to *recognize* and *release* a different aspect of persistent stress which will help lead you toward greater ease and healing. Together with the lessons, you will employ five techniques that have been tailored specifically for the unique challenges of overcoming the effects of stress related to military duty. Each of these techniques is purpose-designed to help you in your careful and scientific analysis of stress in your life. Best of all, altogether the techniques will require less than one hour per day to perform completely.

Now let's take a look at the five BOOTSTRAP techniques that make up this life-changing system:

BOOTSTRAP® TECHNIQUE #1
RECOGNITION SEQUENCE™
(posture sequence)

40 minutes every other day

☑ **RECOGNIZE**
☑ **RELEASE**
☑ **RESTORE**

What you need:

– Quiet space

– Yoga or exercise mat (recommended)

– Computer or MP3 player with speakers

– Recognition Sequence audio recording*

*Download the audio file at **www.bootstrapUSA.com/WIP**
Enter code: X4LQ8*

The purpose of the *recognition sequence* in the BOOTSTRAP system is to provide a forum in which we can explore the various ways we unwittingly add to our level of stress. Remember, you are a scientist attempting to study and understand the workings of stress.

The sequence itself is composed of a series of physical postures borrowed from the practice of yoga. To perform the practice, you'll simply follow along with the instructions on the *recognition sequence* audio recording (available as a free download at www. bootstrapUSA.com/WIP).

By far the most widely-recognized aspect of yoga, these postures are also the most radically misunderstood—even among yoga teachers. Although effective at creating physical flexibility, increasing strength, and even releasing stress (as you'll see), the postures of the *recognition sequence*, when properly performed, have the power to do so much more.

While releasing stress is important, without addressing the underlying causes of its creation, we find ourselves in a never-ending cycle of pressure and anxiety. By helping to illuminate and interrupt the mental and emotional habits that reinforce chronic stress, the postures of the *recognition sequence* have the power to help you learn how to relax your body, soothe your nerves, and calm your mind even in the midst of difficult circumstances.

Stress Fact:

BOOTSTRAP employs five techniques that have been specially designed to combat military-related stress.

It's important to note that the intention here is *not* to perfect the postures. Rather, the sequence serves as a place to study and recognize your self-sabotaging habits, which is a top priority for any self-respecting *stressologist*. This understanding of the workings of stress will set the stage for you to *release* harmful tendencies and *restore* your body and mind to a healthy, well-balanced state. In other words, the *recognition sequence* is not the practice of the BOOTSTRAP process, it is *a place* to practice the BOOTSTRAP process.

At the end of each lesson you will be given specific guidance regarding how to experiment and learn about a particular aspect of the cycle of stress as you perform the sequence. Each week, you will use the *same sequence* of postures to perform *different* experiments. Think of the *recognition sequence* as a set of tools you need to conduct your study of the workings of stress.

Recognition sequence tips:

- Don't eat for an hour prior to practice.
- Practice in comfortable clothing and bare feet.
- Focus on what you're doing, not on reaching a goal; move slowly, be mindful.
- Remember that perfecting the posture is not the goal.
- Keep the weekly lesson in mind.

Remember: Although the recognition sequence looks to be physical exercise, you are merely using it to create situations through which you can learn how stress sneaks into your life. We are using the body to understand the workings of the mind. Think of the sequence as the laboratory where you conduct your research. Each week, you will be assigned different experiments to conduct within the sequence to deepen your understanding while interrupting the processes on which chronic stress relies.

Additional guidance on the recognition sequence can be found in Appendix A, including a series of photographs to assist you in learning the postures.

BOOTSTRAP® TECHNIQUE #2

INTENTIONAL RESTORATION™
(guided relaxation)
40 minutes every other day

☐ **RECOGNIZE**
☑ **RELEASE**
☑ **RESTORE**

What you need:

– Quiet space

– Props to lie comfortably on your back (blankets, pillows, etc.)

– Computer or MP3 player with speakers

– Intentional Restoration audio recording*

*Download the audio file at **www.bootstrapUSA.com/WIP**
Enter code: X4LQ8*

Intentional restoration has the power to release chronic tension, neutralize negative thought patterns, and create a deep, rejuvenating relaxation that stimulates the body's natural healing response. Based on an ancient meditation technique called Yoga Nidra, *intentional restoration* is a little-known technique that has the power to quickly and effortlessly short-circuit the workings of chronic stress.

Performed lying down, you'll use the *intentional restoration* audio recording (available as a free download at www.bootstrapUSA.com/WIP) to guide you through the technique. In each session you will be led,

Stress Fact:

When you're practicing your BOOTSTRAP techniques in your home-based Stress Lab, it's best to select a place that is quiet and relatively free from disturbance.

with eyes closed, to move your attention to various parts of the body. Your task is to simply remain relaxed and focused, and feel whatever sensations are present at the point being named. Let go of analysis, judgment, and internal commentary. It's important to focus on the body, not the mind.

Intentional restoration tips:

Take the time to prepare your space to remove distractions:
- Select a room free from disturbances.
- Lower the lights, but don't turn them off.
- Lie down, but not in bed.

Stay relaxed and at ease:
- Ensure that every part of your body is supremely comfortable.
- Cover yourself with a blanket if cold.
- Remain still, with eyes closed, throughout the technique.
- Stay relaxed, allowing yourself to effortlessly follow instructions.
- Though you're deeply relaxed, resolve to stay awake.
- Don't think about or visualize the points where your attention is guided. Instead, simply feel the sensations present at each point.

Remember: Fundamentally, intentional restoration is not about fixing; rather it's about relaxing the body and the mind so that your natural healing response can take over. Through your commitment, the intentional restoration process, creates healing, ease, and relaxation effortlessly.

IMPORTANT NOTE: *Intentional restoration takes us to the deepest place of relaxation, a place where defensive tensions, suppressed emotions, and repressed memories are free to flow into consciousness. Long-forgotten memories, intense emotions, and even bizarre imagery can arise. This can be unnerving at first, but it's important to recognize that this is part of the process that moves us toward health and well-being. Just relax.*

When disturbing thoughts and emotions come up, they come up to go—let them. Don't invite them to stay by giving them your attention, analyzing where they came from, or asking why they are happening. Simply relax and allow them to move through like clouds through an open sky. If at any time you feel frightened or overwhelmed, simply begin to move your fingers and hands and open your eyes. Come back to the process when you're comfortable.

INSTANT INTERVENTIONS™
as needed

☐ **RECOGNIZE**
☑ **RELEASE**
☑ **RESTORE**

What you need:

– Varies

We all get knocked off balance every now and again. An argument with a loved one, a series of tight deadlines, or a physical illness or injury can all set in motion a cascade of thoughts and emotions that sabotage our days, ruin our sleep, and leave us stressed and anxious.

Instant interventions are designed for just these situations. Unlike our first two techniques, which are designed to be performed in your home-based Stress Lab, *instant interventions* are portable. Whenever you find the mind obsessively thinking about a disturbing event or situation, an *instant intervention* can be used to channel energy away from the disturbing thoughts, thereby interrupting the cycle of stress and helping you to relax. BOOTSTRAP offers four *instant intervention* techniques:

1. Heartfelt Gratitude
2. Focused Walking
3. Victorious Breathing
4. Conscious Sipping

Be sure to review the exact method for the performance of

these important tools. You'll find the complete details of their performance and usage presented in Appendix A at the end of the book.

Instant intervention tips:

- Focus attention like a laser beam.
- Intend to remain undistracted by competing thoughts.
- When you find yourself distracted, immediately return to the technique.

Remember: For the instant intervention to work, you must be fully concentrated on the technique. When distractions from the mind or the environment sidetrack your attention, immediately come back to the technique.

BOOTSTRAP® TECHNIQUE #4
SCIENTIFIC OBSERVATION
5 minutes every other day

☑ **RECOGNIZE**
☑ **RELEASE**
☑ **RESTORE**

What you need:
– Quiet space
– Journal and pen

Chronic stress arises as a result of a tangled web of unconscious reactions, habits, and tendencies. And as we'll see in the coming weeks, many of our best attempts to relieve stress can actually worsen its effects. For this reason, the BOOTSTRAP process invites us to examine our efforts and ask the simple question "How is this working for me?" It's through this process of inquiry that many of the conditions that perpetuate chronic stress and other harmful habits are ultimately undone.

Like any good scientist, you will conduct various experiments and carefully study and document the results. In situations that arise in your *Stress Lab experiments* and your life in general, note how your reactions and habits affect your immediate experience as well as your overall sense of well-being. You'll be asked to spend just five minutes a day noting your observations and conclusions in your Stress Lab journal.

Scientific observation tips:

 – Try to write in your journal at the same time each day.
 – Use the self-study questions in the Stress Lab Experiments section of each week's lesson.
 – Be curious about your progress and how your BOOTSTRAP techniques are affecting your stress levels.

Remember: This practice is not about getting it right. Just write what comes to you regarding the BOOTSTRAP process, the techniques, your experimentation, your stress, and your life. Each week's lesson will include a number of questions to help direct your scientific observation. Review the week's questions each day before journaling. Be curious, not serious.

BOOTSTRAP® TECHNIQUE #5
PERSONAL COMMITMENT
ongoing

☑ **RECOGNIZE**
☑ **RELEASE**
☑ **RESTORE**

What you need:

– Dedication and courage

In the same way that a cancer researcher's personal commitment fuels her breakthroughs in cancer treatment, it is your personal commitment that fuels your movement away from stress and toward greater ease, increased energy, and happiness. For this reason, we ask you to stay connected to your commitment to wholeheartedly engage the BOOTSTRAP system for the next seven weeks.

Each week, spend a few minutes going over that week's lesson. Special effort has been made to make each lesson concise, accessible, and relevant to your life today. Each day, perform your BOOTSTRAP techniques in your home-

Stress Fact:

While the BOOTSTRAP techniques are simple and easily understood, their powerful effects are dependent on two things:

- Daily performance of the techniques

- Purposeful performance of the techniques

Simply performing the techniques is not enough. To obtain maximum benefit, they must be performed with the proper attitude and focus. Remember, the purpose of the exercises is to help us to *recognize, release, and restore.*

based *Stress Lab*. And most importantly, maintain your scientific curiosity. With just a little dedication and effort and in less than an hour a day, you'll make amazing improvements in every aspect of your life.

Personal commitment means:
- Practicing the BOOTSTRAP techniques daily.
- Trying to practice the same time each day.
- Following the guidance in each week's Stress Lab experiments.
- Remaining curiously engaged.

Remember: The BOOTSTRAP process is not supposed to be another source of stress in your life. Your dedication to the process rather than the results will bring lightness, ease, and vitality.

COMMON PITFALLS

There are several common pitfalls that are to be avoided if the BOOTSTRAP process is to be optimally successful:

STRIVING FOR PERFECTION – We all want to get it "right." It's human nature. But this persistent habit will only worsen your stress levels while you're working the BOOTSTRAP process.

The problem is this: At first we may be stressed because of recurring nightmares—we have one source of stress. Then we begin to practice the BOOTSTRAP system and we think we need to get the posture sequence perfect—now we have two sources. We believe we should be completely free from stress already—three sources. We think our *intentional restoration* should be better—four sources. And so on. When we use the BOOTSTRAP process to try to perfect the process, we unwittingly contribute to our stress.

Remember: The cure for this habit of striving for perfection is to do your best *and* relax with the way you are. You make the effort to step up to your potential while relaxing with how things are working out. Put another way, trust in the process. Do your best and leave alone the idea that you should be able to do better.

ENGAGING IN SELF-CRITICISM – A close cousin of striving for perfection is criticizing yourself, and it works to inflame stress in much the same way.

The problem is this: At the heart of self-criticism is the idea that we should somehow be different from how we are. It could be about our physical fitness, our level of patience, or even our stress levels. The moment we believe this idea that we should be different from how we are, we cause conflict—conflict between how we are and how we think we should be. This conflict is yet another source of stress.

Remember: Rather than letting the mind run wild with its constant complaints and comparisons about how you are, try to keep your attention rooted in the moment, in what you're doing. Instead of beating yourself up for missing a day of your BOOTSTRAP practices, let the past go and simply resolve to do better. Relax.

ROTE OR CARELESS PERFORMANCE – Performing the techniques in a haphazard or distracted way will dramatically reduce the effectiveness of the process.

The problem is this: Your chronic stress relies on certain thought patterns for its continued existence. The BOOTSTRAP practices are designed specifically to interrupt these patterns—but this interruption can take place only if you're mentally connected to the practices.

Remember: BOOTSTRAP is using the body to get to the mind.

If the techniques are to pay off, you must involve yourself fully, both mentally and physically. At first, it's normal to have difficulty focusing, but just keep at it. You'll be surprised how quickly you progress.

EMPLOYING A NO PAIN, NO GAIN APPROACH – We all know that if you aren't willing to endure the burn, you'll never become physically fit. And while that is absolutely true in the realm of physical fitness, this same attitude will destroy the effectiveness of your BOOTSTRAP practices—particularly the *recognition* (posture) *sequence*.

The problem is this: "No pain, no gain" as it is applied to the *recognition sequence* assumes that the postures are intended to improve one's physical fitness. But that is simply not true. While there is undoubtedly some physical benefit to doing the sequence, the postures in the BOOTSTRAP system are intended to help us train the mind, not the body.

Remember: As you do the *recognition sequence*, keep in mind that we are not trying to improve physical fitness (although this will undoubtedly happen and is a nice side benefit). Instead, focus on how each lesson provides you with an aspect of stress creation or stress management to explore. Use the postures to investigate the nature of stress and the habits of your mind.

As you'll soon see, engaging in our techniques without indulging in any of the pitfalls is a tall order indeed. Most of us have become expert in all of these habits. In fact, it's the way that we've accomplished virtually all the major achievements in life. Great effort (striving for perfection) combined with a constant evaluation of progress (self-criticism) and a willingness to suffer through trying times (no pain, no gain) is the cocktail for success in nearly all human endeavors. But here it quickly becomes a recipe for worsening our stress instead of overcoming it.

What this means is that we must remain vigilant against these old habits seeping into our practice and undermining the process. In the BOOTSTRAP program, attentiveness and focus, rather than struggle and achievement, are the name of the game. If we are to be successful, we must engage each of the techniques with the utmost level of focus and concentration while remaining free from the pitfalls.

The BOOTSTRAP® Lessons

The final piece to the system is the BOOTSTRAP curriculum. Over the next seven weeks, you will use the BOOTSTRAP techniques to investigate various habits and tendencies that intensify and prolong the cycle of chronic stress. Each week, you will be asked to read a brief lesson exploring one aspect of the chronic stress puzzle, at the end of which will be your daily experiments for that week. As you might imagine, the reading is best done at the beginning of the week to give you time to explore the concepts and solidify your understanding.

Throughout the lessons, we will use an analogy likening life to a movie. This is in no way intended to minimize the experiences in your life or to dismiss them as some Hollywood light show projected on a screen. Not at all. However, in the same way that we have the power to choose how we relate to a movie, we can also choose how we relate to our lives, and the choices we make in this regard affect our experience. Some choices make our situation worse, while others can make it better. Noticing this is part of the *scientific observation* that will empower you to make the choices that interrupt the cycle of stress.

The BOOTSTRAP lessons are presented in three stages, sequenced to help you establish a foundational understanding of how stress is created and then to assist you to master some potent practices designed to restore balance, harmony, and well-being to your life. The lessons are organized as follows:

BOOTSTRAP LESSON OUTLINE

STAGE I: REALITY—THE MOVIE ON THE SCREEN
Lesson 1: What's on the Screen

STAGE II: HARMFUL TENDENCIES—INTENSIFYING THE DRAMA
Lesson 2: The Drama about the Drama
Lesson 3: Complicating the Plot

STAGE III: HELPFUL PRACTICES—ENJOYING THE SHOW
Lesson 4: Focusing on the Screen
Lesson 5: The Opportunity in the Drama
Lesson 6: How to Enjoy a Thriller
Lesson 7: The Tranquil Moviegoer

While the lessons contain powerful techniques and wisdom, let me make one thing clear: _reading the lessons alone is not enough._ This is critical (hence the italic typeface and underline). Remember, the BOOTSTRAP system is designed to work directly on the subtlest aspects of the body and mind, directly and powerfully. Your daily performance of the techniques is the cornerstone of the power of this approach, so please don't skip them.

A Note on Relating to the Lessons

Before we begin, let me briefly say something about the examples you'll find throughout the lessons. While they all may not mirror your own experience, they are all 100 percent relevant to the way chronic stress works in your life.

The reason?

It's because chronic stress is perpetuated through a remarkably predictable and universal progression of events. No matter who you are or what the event triggering your stress may be, the chain reaction that activates the body's stress response unfolds in much the same way. This *stress response* looks like this:

The Stress Response

1. **Experience:** An event is experienced.
2. **Interpretation:** The event is perceived as a threat.
3. **Reaction:** The nervous system initiates the *fight-or-flight response*.
4. **Activation:** Stress hormones are released into the blood system.
5. **Stress:** The feeling of stress is experienced.

While this *stress response* is fairly universal, we must understand that the type of event that triggers it can vary widely from person to person. The familiar example of a car backfire stimulating a memory of combat is a perfect example. While many combat veterans may hear the backfire, only a few may experience a *stress response* around it. And in fact, the same kind of event can affect the same person differently from day to day.

These events, or *stress triggers*, can be situations, sounds, images, smells, tastes, or even thoughts and memories. All that's required is for the nervous system to *interpret* the situation as a threat (*interpret* being the key word here, because no real threat is necessary for the *stress response* to kick in, the nervous system simply must identify the event as such). What's more, a threat doesn't necessarily mean the physical body is imperiled; rather it's simply that one's well-being—physical or mental—is *perceived* to be in jeopardy.

Understanding the difference between the *stress trigger* and the *stress response* will enable you to make the most of the BOOTSTRAP process. As I mentioned, throughout our time together I will use examples to illustrate the workings of the nervous system's *stress response* as well as the techniques for interrupting your chronic stress. These examples are crucial to broadening your knowledge of how chronic stress is fueled and maintained.

Stress Fact:

Stress Fact: Your body's stress response is very similar to everyone else's; the triggers that stimulate your stress response however can be quite unique. Pay attention to the types of situations that trigger your stress. This is a valuable clue to solving your unique stress puzzle.

Of the various examples used here, some of the *stress triggers* will resonate with you and some undoubtedly will not. I've made every effort to use generic and easily relatable examples to illustrate the workings of stress, but please realize that irrespective of whether the example matches your experience, the underlying *stress response* works nearly identically for all of us. In other words, the *stress triggers* given as examples don't need to correspond with the events that trigger your own stress. Just focus on the processes described and you'll come away from the experience with a clear understanding of how the chronic-stress cycle works and how to interrupt it in your own life.

Now you have all the information you need to begin your journey. Remember, one lesson per week, be curious and interested, and practice daily. The BOOTSTRAP process will take care of the rest!

What's on the Screen™
Now is Non-negotiable

LESSON SUMMARY

- *What's on the screen* is a term that refers to what's happening right now.

- *What's on the screen* can't be any different from how it is—at least for *now*.

- *What's on the screen* is non-negotiable.

- *Now is as now is.*

Yogic Source
Satya
(truth)

What's on the Screen™
Now is Non-negotiable

"It is what it is."

You could almost hear the eyes rolling in their sockets as Staff Sergeant Boyle again delivered his now-all-too-familiar motto to his squad members.

It was a searing 120 degrees, and the unit had been baking in this poor excuse for an outpost for the better part of a week. Overtired, under supplied, and peering into an expanse of lifeless, bone-dry desert watching for the telltale evidence of an enemy that never came, the squad was tasked with watching the battalion's flank as the last remnants of resistance were suppressed in the town to their East.

Corporal Ledbetter shook his head. "Come on, Sarge. You know this mission is bogus. There's nothing but snakes and scorpions out on that desert for a thousand miles."

"Yeah, and they told us we'd only be out here two days—tops!" Private Logan whined.

Boyle nodded silently as he scanned the desert through a battered pair of binoculars. To the outside observer, it might seem a game. The grumbling of the squad members about lousy food, questionable *missions, and miserable conditions all of it an attempt to win the unflappable Boyle over to their side.*

But the squad always failed. No matter how compelling, how seemingly well-founded their protests, they were always met with the same familiar motto: "It is what it is."

You see, Boyle through his years of service had learned a simple but often-missed universal truth of life: now is as now is.

At the heart of the BOOTSTRAP process is a single question: *How can I be relaxed now?* And it's a question that is in many ways the key to the stress-management puzzle for two key reasons. First, relaxation is a kind of magic antidote for chronic stress. Look to your own experience and you'll see. When your experience is one of stress, it seems to be defined by a pervading sense of tension—tension in the body and tension in the mind. On the other hand, when an episode of stress has passed, you are left with an overall sense of ease or relaxation, again in both body and mind. No tension, no stress. Relaxation is key.

But the idea that relaxation is an important element in relieving chronic stress is nothing new. It's probably something you've heard a million times. So we won't spend time here with relaxation. Instead we're going to focus on the second, equally important element of this crucial question; one that is usually forgotten. We're going to be focusing on *now*.

Although it is not commonly recognized, *now* is a concept that is almost universally ignored when it comes to finding peace, ease, and relaxation in our lives. While we may think we're concerned with relaxing now, the truth is that our efforts are very often missing this crucial element. And unfortunately, ignoring now is something that carries nasty consequences. Here's how you can check it out for yourself.

Stress Fact:

Now is non-negotiable. Despite how most of us act, what's happening in this moment, no matter what it is, can be no different from how it is—at least for now. And no matter how much you disagree with it, you can do nothing to change it. In the same way that in the moment a tender love scene is projected on the screen of a movie theater, there is no possibility of a bank robbery, a shoot out, or a car chase.

Ask yourself this question: *How can I be relaxed now?* Go ahead. Ask yourself and write down your answer. It needn't be a comprehensive list, just jot down one simple thing that would allow you to be relaxed now. And by the way, if you do feel totally relaxed now, think of a time when you were struggling with a stressful incident and write down what would have made it possible for you to be relaxed in that moment.

When most people do this exercise, their answers focus exclusively on the relaxation piece and all but totally ignore now. Look at your own answer and see if it's not true. If your answer involves *any* kind of change—an improved situation, better life circumstances, a more rewarding job, enhanced health, a happier relationship—it misses the point. At least as far as now is concerned. Why? Because it ignores the fundamental nature of now: *Now is as now is.* Let me explain.

As mentioned in the introduction, life, in some ways, can be likened to watching a movie. When you decide to go see one of the latest Hollywood blockbusters, you have some power over which movie you see, but once the movie starts and is being projected onto the screen, you no longer have any control over what you're seeing, at least in that moment. If in this moment a trailer for a bad horror flick is being projected, that's what you're stuck with;

What is happening now can be no different from how it is—at least not in this moment. *Now is as now is.*

if it's the opening credits, that's what you get; if it's a boring conversation, well, it's a boring conversation, at least for now. The fact is that *what's on the screen* is on the screen. Period. And there's nothing that anyone can do to change it, at least in this moment. In other words: *now is as now is.*

The same is true with *what's on the screen* in your life. At 6:22 and 46 seconds in the morning, it might be your daily commute; at seven minutes and 14 seconds after noon it could be a mouthful of tuna salad; 8:32 and 33 seconds in the evening it might be your living room and the warm glow of the television. Whatever it is, the nature of *what's on the screen* in your life is much the same as the nature of *what's on the screen* in the movie theater. Whether you like it, despise it, are bored by it, or think it to be the greatest thing since sliced bread, there's nothing you can do to change or modify it, not in this moment anyway. It's because *what's on the screen* is non-negotiable, or as Staff Sergeant Boyle would say: *it is what it is.*

It works like this: *What's on the screen* now is you reading these words, in the place you're sitting, with the sounds you're hearing, with the sensations you're feeling. It's just this. *What's on the screen* now, in *this* moment, is you reading these *other* words, and then *these* words. And at some point it will be you putting this book down, but for now, it's you reading *these* words. On and on it goes. And most importantly, because you are reading these words now, there is nothing you can do to change it—at least for now. *What's on the screen* is what it is.

"But wait a minute!" you might say, "I don't have to be reading these words now. I could have decided to watch television instead." And that's true. You *could have* decided (past tense), but the fact is you didn't and here you are, reading. "Well, I could stop reading the lesson and go outside," you may argue. "*Then* outside would be *on the screen*." True enough, but the key word here is *then*. *Then* outside would be *on the screen*, not *now*. You can decide *in the future* to go outside, in a microsecond from now perhaps, and then *what's on the screen* will be your backyard, but for *now*, for this flash of an instant, you're still reading. And so here you are stuck with *what's on the screen*, the non-negotiable now.

To be clear, however, this isn't to say you don't have the ability to influence what's going to be on the screen next—to choose not to read these words, for example. What I am saying is that *in this moment* your ability to choose has no impact because this moment is *already happening*, this moment is already *on the screen*.

It's like this, you can choose to go see *The Big Heist* instead of *The Little Mermaid*—you do have a choice. But once you're seated in the theater and the car chase is on the screen, you have no ability to change that fact *in that moment.* You can get up and walk out in a fraction of a second from now perhaps, but for now, it's the car chase on the screen. Sorry, Ariel.

So when it comes to solving the stress puzzle, we can see that now is an exceedingly important concept, at least on par with relaxation. While it's true that I can seek to be relaxed *when* I have more money, *when* I am home in California, *when* I have a new job, *when* my loved one straightens up and flies right, *what about now?*

"How can I be relaxed now?" might be restated as "How can I be relaxed with *what's on the screen?*" And remember, *what's on the screen* can in no way be different from how it is. It's non-negotiable.

Unfortunately, most of us assume that if we aren't relaxed now, it's *because* of *what's on the screen.* If I could be relaxed now, I would be, the mistaken belief goes. And so, with this logic we don't even try. Instead of considering relaxation now, we look to the future and set ourselves up for the struggle. Rather than creating a life that has us relaxed and happy today, we focus on some imagined future when everything and everybody will live up to our fantasized idea of perfection; a time when job responsibilities will be to our liking, bank accounts will be brimming with cash, and relationships will be free and easy. Ah yes, when all of that happens, *then* I'll be able to relax.

But sadly, there are dire consequences to this strategy. Because by turning our backs on the possibility of relaxation now, in *this*

81

moment, with our sights set on some magically perfect moment in the future, our whole lives become dedicated to *struggling* to create the perfect future while merely *tolerating* the dreadful present. We become happy to be stressed now, so that we can be relaxed when everything finally lines up just right. And unfortunately for most, that storybook future never arrives. Never quite.

With that said, there is nothing wrong with wanting to improve our situations, strengthen our finances, or better our careers. It's perfectly normal to want to lessen traumatic memories, restore physical health, and improve our relationships, but again, *what about now?* What about right now—with *what's on the screen*—how can you be relaxed with this?

The truth is that it *is* possible to do both: to take care of *now* and the future, too. Yet to do this successfully, most of us could use a bit of help with the "taking care of the now" part. This is largely

Our struggle against what's causing us stress in this moment is itself adding to our stress.

because creating relaxation *now* requires a different set of skills than creating it out there in the future.

Where creating future relaxation involves some amount of effort to change, obtain, and achieve, such techniques simply can't work here in the unchangeable now. No, this job requires an entirely different approach. Instead of planning and struggle and control, finding relaxation *here* requires allowing and acceptance, often with situations we don't necessarily like. What this means for the men of Staff Sergeant Boyle's squad is that instead of spending their time griping, grumbling, and groaning about their uncomfortable circumstances—as if all the complaining in the world will do anything to improve their experience anyway—they must work to relax *with* the experience.

A funny thing happens when we shift how we relate to a particular experience. When we recognize that *what's on the screen* is non-negotiable, when we realize that *it is what it is*, when we stop struggling against reality, it's then that relaxation becomes possible. "Relaxation now? In the middle of this hellhole?" Yes, it's possible. All that's required is the cultivation of a new, artful way of being, one that blends control and acceptance in equal measure.

This understanding is a crucial realization when it comes to our health and well-being. Because our struggle against what's causing us stress in this moment is itself adding to our stress.

Baking under the desert sun is bad enough, but when we launch into a tirade of complaints about our conditions and protests over our mission, the only thing that changes is the level of our frustration—which grows. In essence, we engage in dredging up all the details of the unpleasant circumstance while criticizing, judging, and complaining about everything and everybody—and making ourselves sick.

We turn a simple experience of discomfort or intensity into a firestorm of irritation. And none of it changes the fact: it's hot. In any given moment, while we might not be able to make our situation better, we can most assuredly make it *seem* worse. And this is something in which most of us have become experts.

This realization is at the heart of Staff Sergeant Boyle's motto. He recognizes that this moment—*now*—*is on the screen. It is what it is* means to recognize the non-negotiable nature of reality, of this moment. *It is what it is* means to realize how protest against the unchangeable only leads to more irritation. *It is what it is* invites us to forge a new kind of relationship with reality, with *what's on the screen*, one that starves rather than feeds the perpetual cycle of chronic stress.

The invitation here is to experiment with being open to and accepting that which arises in each moment—*while you do your best to improve your circumstance.* It's not helpful to allow yourself to be used as a doormat; it's not appropriate to stay in an unhealthy situation when you can do something about it. So, by all means, stay connected to your intention to live the best life you can. But remember too, that in any moment when you find yourself in an unpleasant circumstance, for that moment, it can be no different.

As we move forward with the BOOTSTRAP process, your ability to recognize the non-negotiable and unchangeable nature of *what's on the screen* will play an important role in restoring your body and mind to a healthy, relaxed state of being.

Here's how you can apply the three-stage BOOTSTRAP process:

RECOGNIZE the nature of this moment, of *what's on the screen*, as unchangeable and non-negotiable, at least for now.

RELEASE your constant focus on the future and the habit of forgetting the possibility of relaxation now; instead consider relaxation with *what's on the screen.*

RESTORE balance and harmony to the body, mind, and nervous system by lessening the struggle against *what's on the screen.*

When you recognize how resistance to *what's on the screen* has no effect on changing *what's on the screen*, you've taken the first step.

Week 1: Stress Lab Experiments™
Now is Non-negotiable

1. RECOGNITION SEQUENCE
*Download the audio file at www.bootstrapUSA.com/WIP   Enter code: X4LQ8

Use the Recognition Sequence audio recording* to perform the sequence once every other day to conduct the following Stress Lab experiment guided by the four-step N.O.T.E. process: Notice, Observe, Try, and Experience.

NOTICE the tendency to act as if *what's on the screen* shouldn't be on the screen.

As you move through the *recognition sequence*, you'll come up against a variety of experiences that you may be convinced should be different from how they are:

"My hamstrings shouldn't be so tight."
"I should be able to balance better than this."
"This sequence is taking forever."

OBSERVE how your opinion about *what's on the screen* has no effect on *what's on the screen*, at least for *this* moment.

All the complaining, criticism, and frustration in the world can have no effect on what you're experiencing *in this moment*. Watch and see.

TRY giving *what's on the screen* your full permission to be on the screen.

Give your hamstrings permission to be tight. Give yourself permission to be a horrible balancer. Give the sequence permission to take its sweet time. Make space for what's on the screen. Don't get confused though, this doesn't mean you should give up. It means to do your best *while* giving *what's on the screen* permission to be here, at least for this moment.

EXPERIENCE the change in your *experience of your experience.*

When we make space for *what's on the screen,* it doesn't change *what's on the screen,* but it does change our experience of it. Where before there was irritation, frustration, or anger, now there's more okay-ness with the moment.

2. INTENTIONAL RESTORATION

*Download the audio file at www.bootstrapUSA.com/WIP   Enter code: X4LQ8

Use the Intentional Restoration audio recording* to perform one session every other day (alternate days with your recognition sequence practice).

3. INSTANT INTERVENTIONS

Use as needed throughout your days (see Appendix A).

4. SCIENTIFIC OBSERVATIONS

Spend five minutes at the end of each day making notations in your journal using the stress-exploration questions below.

– How much of my time and life energy are spent waiting, wishing, or struggling to make things better?

– In what ways am I overlooking the possibility of a sense of peace, ease, and relaxation *now?*

– How does my tendency to abandon the possibility of peace, ease, and relaxation *now* affect my overall life?

– Do I forget that *what's on the screen* is non-negotiable and act as if *this* moment could be different from how it is?

– How are my BOOTSTRAP practices affecting my stress levels, sense of well-being, emotional state, and relationships with others throughout my day?

The Drama about the Drama™

Resistance is Futile

LESSON SUMMARY

- *Resistance* is futile.

- Resisting *what's on the screen* has no effect on changing *what's on the screen.*

- Resisting *what's on the screen* does create mountains of unnecessary suffering and stress.

- *Resistance* is the first *stress intensifier.*

Yogic Source
Parigraha
(grasping)

The Drama about the Drama™
Resistance Is Futile

Icy-cold wind and sheets of unapologetic rain mixed with the deafening whine of jet engines on the flight deck of the USS Carl Vinson. Aircraft recovery operations were always challenging and difficult, at night doubly so. Add to that the winds, rain, and bitter cold of the unforecast squall and misery becomes the defining experience for the blue shirts managing the aircraft on deck—misery in spades.

Despite the protective clothing—the float coats, the cranials, and the foul-weather gear—the noise, the smell, the rain, and the cold were inescapable. Seaman Burke, having had the displeasure of the experience more times than he'd like to remember, grumbled as he donned his equipment in preparation for his shift on deck.

"Tonight is going to really suck," he protested to nobody in particular.

Next to Burke, Chief Petty Officer Washington, was also preparing for the shift. Washington smiled to himself and shook his head. "When you going to learn, Burke?" He gave the young sailor a sideward glance.

"What?" Burke snapped.

"It's mind over matter, man. If you don't mind," Washington said,

cocking his head and throwing up his hands, "it don't matter."

Burke rolled his eyes, "I've heard it a thousand times, Chief, but seriously ... "

"But seriously what?"

"If you don't mind, it don't matter?" Burke shrugged. "I mean, come on, do you honestly think that your quaint saying is going to do anything to take the edge off that nasty squall that's waiting for us outside?"

Washington shook his head. "No, kid, you're looking at it the wrong way. I mean, it's true that a good attitude won't improve the weather, but it's also true that a bad attitude will worsen your experience of the weather—no matter what it is. You've been on this ship long enough to know that."

Petty Officer Washington knew something that any of us could have learned from watching old sci-fi re-runs on TV. It's that the Martians had it right. When, in those 1950s movies, they zipped down to Earth, piled out of their spaceships, pointed their little ray guns in everyone's faces and vaporized anyone who so much as looked at them funny, they warned, "Resistance is futile." And it's true: resistance *is* futile, at least when it comes to stress and your relaxation *now*.

We've already seen how *what's on the screen* can't be any different from what it is, at least not in this moment. Remember, now is non-negotiable:

- If *what's on the screen* is you with a headache, you have a headache.
- If *what's on the screen* has your bank account empty, your bank account is empty.
- If *what's on the screen* has you cooking under 90 pounds of combat gear on a 120-degree day, well, you're cooking.

And no matter how much you struggle against *what's on the*

screen, what's on the screen remains—at least for now.

But it's worse than just that. Because while it's true that our resistance to *what's on the screen* has no impact on changing *what's on the screen,* it does have the effect of making our experience of it worse, less palatable, more irritating, and, yes, more stressful. Despite what you might think, *what's on the screen* is not the source of our suffering. Not at all. Rather, our suffering derives from our *resistance* to *what's on the screen.*

Stress Fact:

Stress intensifiers are habits and tendencies that worsen our stress. The first *stress intensifier* is *resistance:*

When we go to war with *what's on the screen* we only worsen our situation. Remember, now is as now is—at least for now. Your *resistance* only serves to introduce additional conflict and tension.

I don't suffer because of a badly stubbed toe. I don't suffer because of a maddening traffic jam. I don't suffer because an unforecast squall rakes the deck of the Carl Vinson with icy rain and 40-knot winds. No, I suffer because of *how I react* to these situations. It's my *resistance* that creates the *drama about the drama,* and as we'll see, the *drama about the drama* is oftentimes much more unpleasant than the drama itself. What we're pointing toward here is the difference between pain and suffering.

Most of us think of pain and suffering as two ways to describe the same phenomenon. But when we look closely, we see that rather than one phenomenon referred to as either pain or suffering, we instead are faced with two very distinct forces at work. Let's start with pain.

94

The word pain, for our purposes, refers to the actual discomfort caused by an experience—unvarnished and un-interpreted. It's the ache in the stubbed toe, the crawl of the traffic jam, the icy cold of the wind and rain. Ache, crawl, cold. Period. Nothing more and nothing less. Pain includes no frustration, no lament; it doesn't trade in "what ifs" or "should haves." Pain is a simple and inescapable part of moment-to-moment experience. Pain is quite simply the drama that's *on the screen*.

Suffering, on the other hand, is an altogether different kind of animal. In contrast with the *drama on the screen*, which we have learned is fixed, unchangeable, and mandatory, suffering is anything but. Suffering is the anguish, frustration, and irritation that you *add* to an experience—on top of the pain. That's right, I said, *that you add*, meaning that suffering is an option that you yourself manufacture and inject into your experience. Suffering is the *drama we create* about the *drama on the screen*.

Suffering is caused by a single, repetitive thought: *"this should not be like this."*

If suffering is optional anxiety created by our own actions, it only makes sense for us to ask how. And the answer is quite simple, really. Suffering is caused by a single, repetitive thought: *this should not be like this.* It's a direct result of what Chief Petty Officer Washington and, for that matter, the Martians would call *resistance* to *what's on the screen*.

This single repetitive thought, the one that causes so much trouble and angst, comes in many shapes, sizes, and flavors.

Sometimes it sounds like "why me?"; other times "how much longer?"; and still other times "this is ridiculous." But no matter the wording, the underlying sentiment remains the same: *what's on the screen* should be somehow different from *what's on the screen—this should not be like this.* Let's take a look at how it works.

Imagine yourself stuck in a spectacular traffic jam. You're sitting in a seemingly interminable line of cars crawling along at 14 miles per hour in the fast lane. It's a situation that creates considerable irritation and stress for millions of Americans each and every day, for sitting in traffic when you are trying to get somewhere is stressful. Or is it?

While it may be true that most people experience stress and anxiety when trapped in rush-hour gridlock, it's also true that most of that stress and anxiety is self-created. It comes not from the experience but from our *reaction* to the experience; it's not the drama, but the *drama about the drama* that's the culprit. In other words, it's suffering, not pain. Let's look at the experience of being stuck in traffic with fresh eyes—seeing it just as it is.

There you are sitting in a relatively comfortable seat, you're probably listening to some of your favorite music, you have a nice view of the outdoors, and you may even have the cool breeze of the air conditioner wafting over you. This is the situation; this is being stuck in traffic; this is *what's on the screen.* In other words, this is the mandatory, unchangeable "pain" of the experience, which as we can see is really not so bad.

But then something happens when we add our *resistance* to the situation, the moment when we add that single repetitive thought:

this should not be like this. It doesn't matter what specific form the *resistance* takes, as we mentioned before. It may be, "They just built this freeway—couldn't they have added another lane?" It could whine, "I knew I should have taken the surface streets!" It could scheme, "Maybe if I get off at the next exit and take Main Street." But no matter its exact form, the moment the *resistance* arises, our experience changes for the worse. The experience of sitting comfortably and watching the scenery move slowly by is now one of frustration, angst, and dis-ease. We've injected optional, self-created suffering into the experience. This is *the drama about the drama.*

This optional suffering is created through a rather predictable and verifiable process, something we call the *equation of suffering.* It looks like this:

Experience + Resistance = Suffering

To apply it to our example here, our *experience* is the traffic, our *resistance* is our impatience, and our *suffering* is our frustration. Or:

Traffic + Impatience = Frustration

To emphasize, the traffic alone is not the cause of our suffering, despite what many of us believe. In fact, this confusion about the cause of suffering locks us into an inescapable cycle of more and more *optional* misery.

Whenever I believe that traffic = suffering, that being passed over for a promotion = suffering, or that icy-cold weather = suffering, then when any of these events arise in my life, my fate is sealed. Stuck in my automatic and unconscious habit of *resistance,* I unwittingly create *unnecessary* suffering, pile it atop my already-difficult circumstance, and blame it on the world. On the other hand, if I understand how the *equation of suffering* really works, if I can see how it's my reaction to the event that's the cause of my stress and angst, a new possibility arises: namely the prospect of tapping into a relaxed sense of ease and peace right in the middle of the same situations that used to bring me so much anxiety.

Modifying the Equation of Suffering

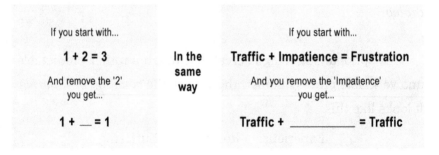

If you start with...

1 + 2 = 3

And remove the '2'
you get...

1 + __ = 1

In the same way

If you start with...

Traffic + Impatience = Frustration

And you remove the 'Impatience'
you get...

Traffic + _____ = Traffic

The way to stop the madness is quite simple. In fact, as anyone who has even the most rudimentary grasp of mathematics can tell you, an equation such as this is quite easily swayed in our favor. Changing the result is simply a matter of changing or removing one element:

If we start with 1 + 2 = 3, we can remove the 2 and get 1 + __ = 1. In the exact same way, when we remove one element from the *equation of suffering,* we dramatically alter the result. If we start with Traffic + Impatience = Frustration, we can remove the impatience and get Traffic + _____ = Traffic (see illustration).

Presto change-o. You're left with just the experience without the nasty taste of irritation and misery, the drama without *the drama about the drama.*

But wait a minute! If modifying the equation and altering the result is so easy, why not get rid of the traffic instead of the *resistance?* After all, without the traffic I'd have neither traffic nor *resistance.* It's a good question and actually points to the failed strategy that most of us embrace.

It's within your power to release your *resistance* to a situation—and if you remove the *resistance,* there's no suffering. It's the BOOTSTRAP® process at work.

When we attempt to modify the equation by wrestling with the traffic (or whatever else may be triggering our *resistance*), we launch ourselves into an unwinnable battle. Why? Because in the moment when we begin to do so, we're working against the universal principle we discussed in lesson number one: now is as now is, a.k.a. *what's on the screen* is non-negotiable.

The traffic can't be removed from the equation because traffic is *what's on the screen;* it can't be modified or influenced in any way. No amount of struggling, striving, whining, or complaining is going to lessen its effect—not in this moment anyway. Would it be nice if the traffic wasn't here? Sure. Would my irritation be reduced if the traffic wasn't here? Absolutely. Is my irritation with the traffic, my complaining about the traffic, my *resistance* to the traffic going to ease the traffic one little bit? Not in *this* moment.

In other words, in this moment I have zero influence over the fact that I am in traffic.

Your habitual and typically unconscious struggle against *what's on the screen* is responsible for a tremendous amount of your stress and anxiety. And this is the good news, because if it's true that your actions are responsible for the mountains of optional suffering in your life, it's also true that your actions can put an end to that optional suffering.

The first step is to become aware of your habits and their results. In this case, it's to tune in to your automatic and unconscious habit of resisting *what's on the screen*. Once you understand how suffering is created and, more importantly, see how you yourself are involved in that process, the way is paved for a new manner of relating to the experiences in your life, a manner that is marked by ease and relaxation rather than struggle and frustration.

In practice it looks like this: if in this moment you are stuck in traffic, you are stuck in traffic (the drama) for this moment, but you are not necessarily stuck with your *resistance* to that traffic (which creates the *drama about the drama*). In other words, while you have no control over the speed of the cars on the freeway, you have tremendous control over how you choose to respond to the speed of the cars on the freeway. It is within your power to *release* your *resistance* to the traffic; you can remove the *resistance* from the equation, and as we've seen above, if there's no *resistance*, there's no suffering.

Here's how you can apply the three-stage BOOTSTRAP process:

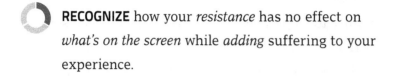 **RECOGNIZE** how your *resistance* has no effect on *what's on the screen* while *adding* suffering to your experience.

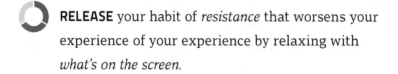 **RELEASE** your habit of *resistance* that worsens your experience of your experience by relaxing with *what's on the screen*.

RESTORE the natural balance and rhythm of the nervous system, the body, and the mind by reducing self-created suffering.

You may already be employing these principles without even knowing it. In fact, the most elite and highly-trained troops throughout the ages have used similar techniques to strengthen their resolve. In my days in the infantry, we had all kinds of sayings (in yoga we would call them mantras) that helped us to release our *resistance*, lessen our suffering, and step up to the challenge at hand. "If it ain't raining, we ain't training," "Pain is simply weakness leaving the body," even Chief Petty Officer Washington's "It's mind over matter: if you don't mind, it don't matter." Of course, at the time I had no idea how these mottos worked; I just knew they worked. But now it's clear that they helped us to embrace our difficult and uncomfortable circumstances (that is, to give up our *resistance*), and with the *resistance* removed from the *equation of suffering*, we were left only with discomfort, only with fatigue, only with what was *on the screen*—the simple drama without the *drama about the drama.*

So, continue to do your best in life: get off the freeway, stand up for what's right, and wholeheartedly chase your dreams. But do so while simultaneously realizing that for now—just now—*what's on the screen* is on the screen and there's nothing you can do about it.

Relax with it, make space for it, give it permission to be as it is *while simultaneously* using your talents, your drive, and your ingenuity to move toward an even more fulfilling future. As a great Zen master once said, "Accept what is as it is, *and* help it to be its best." Relaxed and at ease all along the way.

Remember, the Martians had it right: resistance *is* futile.

Week 2: Stress Lab Experiments™
Resistance Is Futile

1. RECOGNITION SEQUENCE
Download the audio file at www.bootstrapUSA.com/WIP   Enter code: X4LQ8

Use the Recognition Sequence audio recording* to perform the sequence once every other day to conduct the following Stress Lab experiment guided by the four-step N.O.T.E. process: Notice, Observe, Try, and Experience.

NOTICE your habit of *resistance* as it seeps into your performance of the *recognition sequence*.

As you move through the sequence, you will invariably come up against experiences the mind doesn't like. When *what's on the screen* doesn't meet the mind's expectations, pay attention to how you are automatically thrown into *resistance* to the experience or circumstance.

Here's a tip: when on the lookout for *resistance*, don't look for *resistance* but instead for negative emotions like frustration, impatience, or anger. Trace these emotions back to the cause. This so-called cause is probably what you're resisting.

OBSERVE how your *resistance* to *what's on the screen* has no effect on what's happening now, but adds suffering on top of what's happening now.

When *what's on the screen* is bad balance, your experience will be one of bad balance. When, however, bad balance is resisted, you get bad balance *plus* frustration, angst, and struggle. Watch how either way you get bad balance, at least in *this* moment. The same is true for all experiences.

TRY releasing your *resistance*.

Instead of allowing your habit of unconscious and automatic *resistance* to run the show, decide to experiment with releasing your *resistance* to *what's on the screen*, if only for a few moments.

For ten seconds, relax with bad balance, make friends with tight hamstrings, make space for discomfort. Give *what's on the screen* your full permission to be how it is.

EXPERIENCE how your experience of *what's on the screen* improves as *resistance* is released.

Nothing in your experience has changed. *What's on the screen* is still on the screen. But look, something *has* changed: your experience of your experience, of *what's on the screen.* Without the *resistance*, it's different, improved. Discovering how your relationship to an experience can dramatically affect your stress is an important discovery. Congratulations!

2. INTENTIONAL RESTORATION

*Download the audio file at www.bootstrapUSA.com/WIP   Enter code: X4LQ8

Use the Intentional Restoration audio recording* to perform one session every other day (alternate days with your *recognition sequence* practice).

3. INSTANT INTERVENTIONS

Use as needed throughout your days (see Appendix A).

4. SCIENTIFIC OBSERVATIONS

Spend five minutes at the end of each day using the self-study questions below to make notations in your journal.

– How often do I automatically resist difficult, disappointing, or uncomfortable situations?

– How does my *resistance* to *what's on the screen* affect my stress level?

– Am I able to discern between the pain inherent in an event and the self-created *suffering* I contribute to it?

– How are my BOOTSTRAP practices affecting my ability to remain relaxed without *resistance?*

– How are my BOOTSTRAP practices affecting my stress levels, sense of well-being, emotional state, and relationships with others throughout my day?

Complicating the Plot™
The Problem of Disintegration

LESSON SUMMARY

- *Disintegration* is the state of mental distraction and conflict.

- *Integration* is the state of mental focus and wholeness.

- *Disintegration* is caused by a wandering focus.

- *Disintegration* is the second *stress intensifier.*

Yogic Source
Vikshepa
(distraction)

Complicating the Plot™
The Problem of Disintegration

Crack!

The sound of the sniper rifle was followed two seconds later by the telltale cloud of dust created by the impact of the .50 caliber round on the target 1,500 yards down range. Corporal Scully confirmed the "kill" through his M49 spotting scope, though Sergeant Martinez knew the moment he squeezed the trigger that his round would find its mark. He rolled up to sitting and laid down his M107 sniper rifle on the poncho beside him.

"It's like that." Martinez said to Scully.

Scully nodded. "I swear I'm doing everything you are."

"Except hitting the target." Martinez quipped.

"Yeah, except that." Scully paused. "That and that thing you're doing with your eyes."

"What thing with my eyes?" Martinez frowned.

"You know, when you close your eyes once you're in firing position."

Martinez shook his head. "That's not about my eyes, Scully; it's about my breath."

"Oh, I take the deep breaths like I was taught..."

"It's not just that," Martinez interrupted.

"What do you mean?"

"It's about breath, but it's even more about mind," Martinez said. "When I first lie down, I have to clear my head. I've got all sorts of distractions living up there: concerns about the mission, anxiousness about remaining concealed, worries about my wife and kids at home, and on and on."

"What does your breath have to do with all that?"

"I use it as a tool to draw me into a kind of single-pointedness. It's what I call 'the key to the kill.' " Martinez slid out of the way and motioned toward the rifle. "Give it a try."

Scully lay down and took up a firing position, aiming the M107 downrange.

"Close your eyes and notice how there are all sorts of thoughts and ideas and concerns up there," Martinez said.

Scully, eyes closed, nuzzled his cheek into the stock of the weapon.

"Now bring your attention to your breath. Really. Fully. Breathe slowly and deeply while you focus on the breath. Feel it as it moves through your nostrils with 100 percent of your attention."

Scully nodded.

"Like a laser beam of attention," Martinez said. "Keep it there. Don't let it wander."

Martinez allowed a few seconds to pass.

"Now stay relaxed, let your eyes open, and focus that same one-pointed attention downrange."

Crack!

Martinez confirmed the "kill" through his spotter scope.

Scully looked up, a big grin etched on his face. "It works!"

"So the problem wasn't steadying the rifle as much as it was steadying your mind, huh?"

"I guess you're right, Sarge."

Martinez had recognized one of the marksman's great secrets: a perfect shot starts not with a steady rifle but with a steady mind. If you wrestle directly with the rifle, without first steadying the mind, you'll likely end up with a shot that falls far from its mark. Why? It's because the mind controls the rifle *through* the body. If you wish to fix an erratic aim, you can't simply wrestle with the poorly aimed rifle or the shaky hand, as these are mere symptoms of a deeper problem—in this case the unsteady mind.

Solve the underlying problem and the symptoms go away. It's an eternal law and one that we all intuitively embrace in most areas of our lives. But when we focus on the *symptoms* while ignoring the *problem,*

Stress Fact:

Disintegration is the second *stress intensifier* responsible for creating unnecessary frustration and angst in our lives. Think of disintegration as multi-tasking run amok. When our attention is divided among various competing priorities, our experience is negatively affected. As a result of disintegration, we begin to feel internally conflicted and stressed.

that's a strategy that simply doesn't work. Anyone can tell you that treating the headache (symptom) and ignoring the brain tumor (problem) is a bad move. And in the same way, if we wish to be successful in improving our aim, we must address not simply the poor aim (symptom) but also the unsteady mind (problem).

Believe it or not, the same is true whether we're aiming for a target downrange or aiming for the cure to chronic stress. Where in marksmanship an unsteady mind can cause a wobbly aim, in the cycle of stress the unsteady mind can cause the creation of truckloads of unnecessary angst and tension. These habits actually obstruct the body's natural healing response while keeping the nervous system over-stimulated, the body wracked with tension, and our lives firmly entrenched in anxiety, frustration, and struggle. But we don't have to live this way.

In yoga we have a term to denote total presence. It's a state that is free from criticism and worry, it lacks any thought of the future or the past, and it involves every part of our beings: our body, our energy, and the fourteen or so people who seemingly live in our heads. It's the state athletes call being "in the zone." We call it *integration.*

In the movie theater of life, *integration* means to be fully connected to *what's on the screen*, to be engrossed in *this* story line, absorbed in the here and now. If *what's on the screen* is a loved one telling you about her day, *integration* means being fully engaged with your loved one. If *what's on the screen* is writing a paper for school, *integration* means being fully devoted to the writing. If *what's on the screen* is mowing the lawn on a hot summer's day, *integration* means to be fully absorbed in the mowing, step by step, row by row. Just this. Here. Now. And when we're integrated, we have an experience that's satisfying, engaging, fulfilling.

Not surprisingly, *disintegration* is the opposite of *integration.* Disintegration is a potent *stress intensifier* that can ruin not just a movie but a life. While in the integrated state, I'm fully engaged with the task at hand—with every aspect of body and mind. When *disintegrated,* I'm anything but. Instead of being immersed in just the here and now, the *movie on the screen,* the habit of *disintegration* has me *complicating the plot* by adding all kinds of additional disturbances. In addition to the movie, my attention flits between the green glow of the exit lights, the sound of the teenager crunching her popcorn behind me, my worries about all the things I have to do tomorrow, and the argument I had with a friend earlier in the day. *Disintegration* is a state that is caused by a mental habit that distracts us from the simplicity of *what's on the screen;* it's a habit that complicates our experience while creating internal conflict and intensifying stress with debilitating results. Where *integration* is simple and calm, *disintegration* is complicated and conflicted.

Worse yet, for many of us, *disintegration* has seeped into virtually every aspect of our lives. For most, the problem begins first thing each morning: When the alarm goes off, it's time to get up—*simple.* But then you may have thoughts like "I don't want to get up. Can't I just sleep a few more minutes? Maybe I don't really need to take a shower this morning. Couldn't I call in late?"—*complicated.* You're driving to work and the freeway traffic is moving 14 miles per hour—*simple*. "I can't believe this traffic. They should just widen the freeway. Why don't these people take transit? I'm going to be late. I knew I should have taken the surface streets"—*complicated*. And on and on it goes throughout the day and every day. Complications and conflict are invited, even actively encouraged, through our untrained, unbridled wandering minds. It's our unconscious habit of *disintegration* at work. Without even recognizing it, we complicate the simple plot of *what's on the screen* by adding additional story lines in the form of worries and distractions and regrets and complaints.

From this you can see how *disintegration* is the enemy of our well-being. Our distracted focus complicates the here and now by conjuring memories of past trauma, projecting troublesome "what-if" scenarios, and creating all manner of mental and emotional disturbances, each of which can have the effect of intensifying our stress.

Based on our description of *disintegration*, for some of us, it may seem as if this is where we live all the time. It may even seem as if *integration*—the experience of calm, one-pointed focus, free from the distraction of the wandering mind—is an impossible goal. But actually most of us are able to create this sought-after state rather regularly. Just think of the one thing you love to do more than anything else, the thing you read about, dream about, the thing you arrange your weekends and vacations around. It may be skiing, it could be mountain climbing, it might be painting, gardening, listening to music, or spending time with friends. It could be anything. Whatever it is, bring it to mind. Now close your eyes and think about what your experience is like in your peak moments of engaging in that activity. Take your time. Notice that in those moments there's no thought about what you need to do back at work. There's no concern for what you did yesterday. There's an absence of memories from the past and worries for the future. There's no sense of criticism or judgment about your performance. There's no worry about how long you'll be engaged in the activity, there's not really even a sense that you're doing the activity. You're *engrossed* in the experience, lost in the moment. You feel whole, fulfilled, at ease, happy. This is *integration*.

The Simplicity of Integration

The Complication of Disintegration

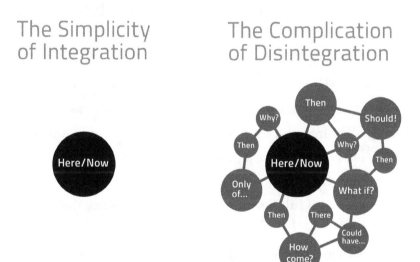

Through integration, you become immersed in *what's on the screen*. The awkward efforts to maneuver yourself down a crowded snow-covered mountain with two boards strapped to your feet becomes skiing. The fumbling attempt to play an intricate series of chords on your guitar becomes music. The clumsy struggle to perform complex steps in time with music becomes dancing.

Believe it or not, the powerful effect of *integration* is even what makes our experience with video games so engaging.

In each of the above examples, *integration* simplifies our experience, merging the diverse components of the activity into a fulfilling whole. It's an experience where even the sense of you as

> **Happiness isn't caused by your favorite activity; happiness is caused by *integration*...by how much *what's on the screen* happens to integrate you.**

separate from the activity disappears. Rather than "I am skiing," it's just skiing. Instead of "I am playing the guitar," it's just music. Rather than "I am dancing," it's just dancing. In the same way that we are pulled into and even lost in an actual movie in a theater, through *integration* we are pulled into and lost in the experience of the moment—the *movie on the screen* of life. And with this arises a profound sense of fulfillment and ease, an experience that we call happiness.

What this means is that happiness isn't caused by your favorite activity; happiness is caused by integration. Happiness isn't caused by *what's on the screen*; happiness is caused by how much *what's on the screen* happens to integrate you. No integration, no happiness. It's just that's simple.

Now here's the valuable take-away: If my happiness relies not on circumstance, not on *what's on the screen*, but on *integration*, this opens up an unprecedented opportunity. If I can learn how to be integrated no matter *what's on the screen*, I can find happiness and ease in all kinds of circumstances—and happiness and ease are definite antidotes for stress. So, is it possible? You bet. And that's why cultivating the skill to remain integrated, present, and engaged with just *what's on the screen* is so valuable.

The BOOTSTRAP process challenges us to learn how to create the same sense of *integration* we get from our favorite activities, in most any setting. What if you could get the same intoxicating experience you get from skiing without ever setting foot on the mountain? What if you could invite the same sense of satisfaction you get from fishing while sitting behind your desk at work? What if you could become immersed in *this* moment in the same way you do when listening to your favorite piece of music right here, right now?

The answer is that you would have access to an unbounded sense of satisfaction and fulfillment—a kind of *portable* happiness and ease. One that you could access no matter where you are or what you're doing. One that would dismantle and destroy the process that keeps you trapped in the cycle of chronic stress. This is precisely what you'll investigate this week in your Stress Lab.

My invitation to you this week is to dive into the investigation of the debilitating habit of *disintegration* during your Stress Lab experiments and your daily life.

Here's how you can apply the three-stage BOOTSTRAP process:

RECOGNIZE how your distracted focus and unsteady mind, wandering to past events, worrying about possible outcomes, and criticizing your circumstance, *complicates* your experience and adds to your stress.

RELEASE the habit of focusing on the distractions in the mind and mentally wandering away from your current experience.

RESTORE a healthy balance in both body and mind as the complication of *disintegration* is replaced by the simplicity of *integration*.

Take a page out of Sergeant Martinez's playbook and go to the source of the problem rather than chasing after symptoms. Use your practices to train yourself to focus on the here and now, on just *what's on the screen*. The results will surprise you.

Week 3: Stress Lab Experiments™
The Problem of Disintegration

1. RECOGNITION SEQUENCE
Download the audio file at www.bootstrapUSA.com/WIP   Enter code: X4LQ8

Use the Recognition Sequence audio recording* to perform the sequence once every other day to conduct the following Stress Lab experiment guided by the four-step N.O.T.E. process: Notice, Observe, Try, and Experience.

NOTICE the tendency of the mind to wander from the here and now, from *what's on the screen*.

Despite your intention to focus on the performance of the *recognition sequence*, the mind wanders. Criticizing, commenting, comparing, and complaining are just a few of the untrained mind's favorite activities. Be curious and really notice the habit.

OBSERVE the effects of the wandering mind and how it creates *disintegration* and *complicates the plot*.

The arms are fatigued? It's just sensation. Balance unsecure? It's just one foot off the floor, both feet on the floor, repeat. Legs tight? It's just restriction. It's simple. That is, until we begin to *complicate the plot* through *disintegration*.

The never-satisfied mind gets ahold of the experience and through its "shoulds" and "what if's" and endless distracted thoughts, it shifts the experience from the simplicity of the *movie on the screen* to a complicated and conflicted mess of impatience, criticism, frustration, and struggle.

TRY rooting attention in the here and now, on just *what's on the screen*, ruthlessly and without compromise.

Devote the full force of your attention to feeling the sensations in the body. Resolve to keep the mind present with your physical experience. When you find yourself drifting to thoughts or daydreams, into the past or future, immediately bring yourself back. Focus and feel.

EXPERIENCE the effects of reining in the mind, of focusing on just *what's on the screen*.

Observe the move from the complication of *disintegration* to the simplicity of *integration*. Note how your experience changes. Calm, ease, just this.

2. INTENTIONAL RESTORATION

*Download the audio file at www.bootstrapUSA.com/WIP   Enter code: X4LQ8

Use the Intentional Restoration audio recording* to perform one session every other day (alternate days with your *recognition sequence* practice).

3. INSTANT INTERVENTIONS

Use as needed throughout your days (see Appendix A).

4. SCIENTIFIC OBSERVATIONS

Spend five minutes at the end of each day using the self-study questions below to make notations in your journal.

– How often do I find myself engaged in one activity but thinking of other things?

– In what ways do I encourage *disintegration* (intentionally daydreaming, mentally escaping from the moment, etc.)?

– How does it feel, physically and emotionally, when I'm pulled in several directions as a result of disintegrating tendencies?

– How are my BOOTSTRAP practices affecting my stress levels, sense of well-being, emotional state, and relationships with others throughout my day?

Focusing on the Screen™
The Practice of Conscious Feeling™

LESSON SUMMARY

- *Disintegration* causes complication and conflict; *integration* causes clarity and ease.

- *Conscious feeling* is a tool to help us cultivate *integration*.

- *Conscious feeling* involves focusing on bodily sensations, whole-heartedly and unerringly.

Yogic Source
Dharana
(concentration)

Focusing on the Screen™
The Practice of Conscious Feeling™

"Focus, ... I guess."

Staff Sergeant Delgado looked past the radio stack at Airman First Class Bremerton, who sat looking out the windshield of the armored Humvee.

"That's the best answer you can come up with, Tammy?" Delgado placed her Kevlar helmet on her head. "I've never seen anyone with nerves like yours—hell, you make most of the guys look like sissies."

Bremerton, a diminutive blonde and former cheerleader from a small West Texas town, just shrugged. She sat staring blankly out the windshield, practically swallowed whole by her body armor and helmet. The fact is that she never really contemplated the question before: what was her secret for staying so relaxed on these dangerous convoy missions?

They were minutes away from rolling out the gates on another late-night, high-speed convoy run to the outskirts of Baghdad. The threat of enemy attack by ambush or improvised explosive device

(IED) was a constant companion any time they were outside the wire, and as usual, it had just about everybody's nerves on end.

"It must be more than that. You must have some secret," Delgado prodded.

Bremerton just looked back toward her friend.

"But it can't just be focus," Delgado continued. "Heck, I'm focused. I couldn't be more focused. I'm focused on what might happen around the next curve, I'm focused on thinking about what could happen if we're ambushed, I'm focused on worrying about where IEDs might be planted."

Bremerton shook her head. "It's not quite like that. It's a focus on what is happening instead of on what could be happening." She paused to think. "Yeah, that's it. It's like I'm fully occupied with the job at hand, I'm feeling the road through the steering wheel in my hands, watching all the details of the route as it unfolds ahead of us, tracking the line of taillights in the darkness ... "

"That's it?" Delgado seemed less than satisfied with the answer.

Bremerton nodded silently to herself and looked back to Delgado "Yeah, that's it. It's a bit strange, I suppose, but it's like my intense focus on what is happening seems to push all of the frightening thoughts about what could happen out of my head."

"So you're spacing out?"

Bremerton thought for a moment. "No, it's not that at all. In fact, my awareness of my surroundings is heightened. It's like I'm about to shoot a game-winning three pointer in the last seconds of a basketball game. I see my teammates, I'm perfectly aware of the other team's players, but I'm not distracted. It's like..."

"...you're 'in the zone'?"

"Yeah, exactly like that."

Interesting thing about our attention: it can focus on only one thing at a time. And while I know that this claim may seem an unlikely fact in our multitasking world, it's one that has been scientifically proven by neuroscientists at the Massachusetts Institute of Technology. Laboratory experiments have verified that while you may think you're paying attention to many things around you at one time, you're actually just switching between things very rapidly. Think of it as changing channels on your television: it's possible to flip from one show to another with astonishing quickness, but you can only ever have one show on the screen at a time. If you're watching the Nature Channel, you can't be watching the Military Channel.

When it comes to your attention, multitasking is a myth. But in truth this is good news because this seeming limitation of attention is at the same time a tremendous opportunity for us. And as Airman Bremerton learned in Iraq, it can be leveraged to help stop the accumulation of unnecessary stress and anxiety in its tracks.

Where the last lesson was about the complication caused by *disintegration*, this week we're exploring how to create its opposite: the helpful state of *integration*. One way we do this in the BOOTSTRAP process is by applying a technique called *conscious feeling*. As you may have noticed, a lot of emphasis is placed on feeling in a number of our techniques. And as with everything in our process, it's no accident.

The reason for placing such emphasis on *conscious feeling* is that, when done properly, it serves as a powerful antidote to the stress-causing tendencies of *disintegration* and *resistance*. We've seen how both *disintegration* and *resistance* are unconscious habits of the mind that can pollute our experience with unnecessary irritation. When the mind launches into a stubborn battle with *what's on the screen*, we get thrust headlong into the cross fire. When the mind is busily obsessing about the 34 things

Stress Fact:

Conscious feeling can interrupt the cycle of chronic stress quickly and powerfully. However two main stumbling blocks can sabotage the effectiveness of the technique.

Thinking about Feeling: Feeling is different from thinking—and for interrupting the cycle of stress, thinking has a very different effect. Remember: if what you are focusing on is experienced in words, ideas, images, or concepts, you're thinking, not feeling. Feeling is pure bodily sensation, before we put labels or words to the experience.

Lax Focus: In order for *conscious feeling* to be the most effective, your attention must be steadily focused and with as little distraction as possible. Think of the intense focus of a laser beam. At first this may seem impossible, but with practice, focus will grow as will the technique's effectiveness in fighting stress.

it has to do in the next hour, we get dragged right along into that drama. When the mind projects Technicolor images of a past ordeal, we find ourselves seated for the show, front row center. And as we've seen, the consequences of each of these habits of the mind are more stress, more angst, and a diminished sense of happiness and ease.

Conscious feeling works by interrupting these damaging habits and robbing them of the energy they need to function, which is why it is central to our techniques for helping us *enjoy the show*. While the practice itself is deceptively simple, it still packs a wallop that can stop the unnecessary continuance of the cycle of chronic stress in its tracks.

Conscious feeling works by interrupting these damaging habits and robbing them of the energy they need to function

Let's begin our investigation with a discussion about what the technique looks like. For a lot of us, the word *feeling* conjures the thought of emotions—*feeling* sad, *feeling* happy, *feeling* anxious. However, here we are referring to another kind of feeling, the feelings we might think of as bodily sensations, such as tingling and pulsing, heat and coolness, and heaviness and lightness. *Conscious feeling* asks you to simply shine your attention on these sensations as they are felt in the body. At times you may be asked to experience all the sensations in the body simultaneously; at others you may be guided to sense the sensations at a single point. Regardless, your task is to focus on the raw, unprocessed experience of the body as felt in skin and muscle—the felt sense in the body.

A surprising number of people find the technique challenging at first. And for those having difficulty, two main stumbling blocks seem to be the chief saboteurs of the technique: *thinking about feeling* and *lax focus*. Let's look at each in turn.

Thinking about Feeling: Feeling is different from thinking. And early on it's common to have difficulty discerning between *feeling* a particular sensation and *thinking* about that same sensation. In other words, thinking about the sensation *in your mind* can be easily mistaken for feeling the sensation *in your body*.

Let's try an experiment. Close your eyes and think about your right knee. Visualize your knee; imagine its shape and color and size. Now notice how that thought about your knee is occurring in a particular location (for me the thought floats up and slightly to the right of my head, much like a thought balloon in a comic strip). Now let go of that thought and bring your attention to your right knee (you may want to tap or pinch your knee so you have a distinct sensation to work with). Once you're focused on the sensation, the *actual experience* happening in the knee right now, notice how the sensations that are happening in the knee also have a particular size, shape, and location—and it's a location that's decidedly different from the location of the *thought* about the knee. You can now go back to the thought to verify this.

To put this all another way, the *thought* about your knee and the *sensation* in your knee are two completely different experiences. Just as your thought about a loved one is different from your actual loved one, so it goes with your thought about sensations and the actual sensations. And while the difference between a thought and a feeling may seem unimportant, the fact is that thinking about sensation does nothing to neutralize stress-producing *resistance* and *disintegration.*

If my attention is wholly consumed by the details of this moment, I don't have the capacity to worry about what might happen tomorrow.

The whole purpose of *conscious feeling* is to interrupt the process through which the mind creates unnecessary worry, anxiety, and stress. And because the mind creates these negative feelings through thinking, you must disentangle yourself from thought and focus exclusively on your physical experience of sensation, or just *what's on the screen* in this moment, to successfully derail the process. To *consciously feel* means to do so in a non-verbal, non-mental way; to feel sensation free from labels, ideas, and personal preferences. Keep in mind: if the experience of feeling is coming in words, pictures, images, or ideas, it's not feeling. It's thinking. When you find yourself focused on thoughts about a sensation, simply reorient back to the sensation itself.

Lax Focus: This is the second potential snare and has to do with the intensity of our concentration. To be effective, *conscious feeling* must be practiced with a focus that is at once pointed and unerring; your total attention has to be placed on these sensations with the intensity and focus of a laser beam and without deviation. A good-enough approach just won't do. The reason for this has to do with how the practice of feeling works to derail the habits that perpetuate and aggravate our stress and anxiety.

It works like this: since attention can focus on only one thing at a time, if we are able to focus exclusively on one thing without deviation, we can effectively keep harmful and disintegrating thoughts out of our awareness. If my attention is wholly consumed by the details of this moment, I don't have the capacity to worry about what might happen tomorrow.

Have you ever been worried about a work situation? Maybe an argument with your boss or an avalanche of tight deadlines? Imagine yourself at home doing some chores, and even though it's the weekend, you find your day consumed and poisoned by worry about your work problems. As you hang a picture on the wall, a poorly-aimed swing of the hammer misses the nail and smashes your thumb.

"Ouch!"

You drop the hammer and the nail, and all your attention is immediately consumed by the burning and throbbing in your thumb. In that moment, and for as long as your thumb aches, your work problem no longer bothers you. Why is that? Did your circumstances change? Did your work issue resolve itself? No. It's just that once you hit your thumb, all your attention focused on the feeling in your thumb and—abracadabra—your work problems stopped nagging you.

Now, of course, I'm not advocating you mash your thumb with a hammer every time you find yourself dwelling on stress-creating thoughts, but understand the underlying point. When attention is directed away from unhelpful thoughts, they lose their power over us. Now you just need to learn how to do this without resorting to the use of a hammer, a brick, or some other finger-flattening device!

Let's return to our movie-watching example for a moment. Put yourself back in the theater and imagine that the long-awaited summer blockbuster has just begun. Just as quickly as the movie begins, you're propelled into the world of the characters, the story lines, and plot. Left behind is the world of the auditorium, your worries about your job, your financial concerns, and every other aspect of your life. Because your attention is *fully invested* in the *movie on the screen,* everything else is, in a way, pushed out of your awareness. This is why movies are the great escape from the pressures of daily life; through the power of *integration*, they harness the mind in a way that keeps it from creating mischief and misery.

Now let's look at Airman Bremerton's example. Many of us know, or at least can imagine, the angst and fear that can arise during a combat mission. It's a fear that can become overwhelming and paralyzing, and it's one that is often fueled by the mind's replaying of "what-if" scenarios involving ambushes, destruction, and death. If we can occupy the mind with positive or even neutral thoughts, the harmful thoughts that spawn worry, fear, and anxiety can be minimized or even pushed out altogether. Recall Airman

Bremerton's words:

> "It's a focus on what is happening instead of on what could be happening. It's like I'm fully occupied with the job at hand, I'm feeling the road through the steering wheel in my hands, watching all the details of the route as it unfolds ahead of us, tracking the line of taillights in the darkness."

Her intense focus on just *what's on the screen,* just what's happening now, occupies her attention in a way that pushes out *disintegration, resistance,* and other harmful thought patterns. It's a method that can work with troubling memories, frustrating worries, and other angst-producing thoughts. And it's something you can experience and develop in your Stress Lab.

Here's how you can apply the three-stage BOOTSTRAP process:

RECOGNIZE how the intense focus of *conscious feeling* can positively affect your sense of well-being in any given moment.

RELEASE the tendency to allow attention to wander unmanaged and unsupervised.

RESTORE your body and mind's natural relaxed state by withdrawing your participation from unhelpful patterns of thought.

Do this first in your performance of the *recognition sequence,* and as you gain skill with the technique, move the practice of *conscious feeling* into mildly stressful situations such as traffic or an argument with a co-worker. As your ability to feel—wholeheartedly and without deviation—grows, over time you will be able to move on to the heavy lifting in life, such as conflicts in your closest relationships, your health challenges, or traumatic past events.

Little by little, your capacity for *conscious feeling* builds along with your ability to interrupt the harmful stress-inducing tendencies that poison your life.

Week 4: Stress Lab Experiments™
The Practice of Conscious Feeling

1. RECOGNITION SEQUENCE
Download the audio file at www.bootstrapUSA.com/WIP   Enter code: X4LQ8

Use the Recognition Sequence audio recording* to perform the sequence once every other day to conduct the following Stress Lab experiment guided by the four-step N.O.T.E. process: Notice, Observe, Try, and Experience.

> **NOTICE how *resistance* to *what's on the screen* creates unnecessary frustration and anxiety.**
>
> Your Stress Lab experiments might be interrupted by a lawn mower outside the window, a pet scratching at the door, children wanting attention. You may snap with frustration: "Can't you see I'm busy trying to get rid of my stress!" Remember, all of it is *what's on the screen,* and resisting any part will yield the same predictable result: stress. Check it out for yourself.
>
> **OBSERVE how *disintegration* destroys the simplicity of *what's on the screen* and complicates your experience with thoughts, opinions, and criticisms.**
>
> Any of these sound familiar?
>
> > *"I really don't have time for this sequence today."*
> >
> > *"I can't believe I'm still having problems with this shoulder."*
> >
> > *"Did I turn the oven off?"*
>
> Who invited these never-satisfied strangers into the theater? More importantly, feel the complicating and conflicting effect they have on your experience of this moment.
>
> **TRY short-circuiting the *stress intensifiers* with a laser-like focus on bodily sensations: *conscious feeling*.**
>
> Cultivate a ruthless laser beam of attention focused on bodily sensations. Each time attention wanders from feeling into thinking, simply bring it back. No compromise.

136

EXPERIENCE the simplicity, calm, and ease present in the moments when you're focused on just this, *what's on the screen.*

Where did the effects of *resistance* vanish to? What happened to the complications from *disintegration*? No need to struggle against *resistance* or *disintegration* just focus like a laser beam and the habits evaporate. Pretty cool, eh?

2. INTENTIONAL RESTORATION

*Download the audio file at www.bootstrapUSA.com/WIP   Enter code: X4LQ8

Use the Intentional Restoration audio recording* to perform one session every other day (alternate days with your *recognition sequence* practice).

3. INSTANT INTERVENTIONS

Use as needed throughout your days (see Appendix A).

4. SCIENTIFIC OBSERVATIONS

Spend five minutes at the end of each day using the self-study questions below to make notations in your journal.

– Am I able to consciously feel wholeheartedly, without deviation, for more than a few moments?

– Am I being ruthlessly honest with myself about how completely I'm focusing on feeling during my *recognition sequence* and other Stress Lab experiments?

– How might the practice of *conscious feeling* reduce the creation of stress and anxiety?

– What are some "light" situations in my everyday life, outside my Stress Lab, with which I might begin to experiment with *conscious feeling?*

– Do I have any mental habits that may be sabotaging my ability to consciously feel?

– How are my BOOTSTRAP practices affecting my stress levels, sense of well-being, emotional state, and relationships with others throughout my day?

Drama and Opportunity™
Building Capacity

LESSON SUMMARY

- Life's challenges are *opportunities* to build our capacity for ease-filled living.

- The challenge of life's difficulties can be used to build the capacity of our mental and emotional selves.

- The more mental and emotional capacity you create, the more peace and ease in your life—in all kinds of circumstances.

Yogic Source
Tapas
(burning effort)

Drama and Opportunity™
Building Capacity

"I'm not like you, Gunny," Private Mitchell protested under the weight of his combat gear. "All this punishment—it's not my thing. I just don't like it."

Gunnery Sergeant Hernandez dropped his rucksack into the sand and shot Mitchell a look. "Like? Did you say like?"

"Yeah, Gunny, ... like."

"You think I like this stuff?" he barked.

Mitchell shrugged. "Sure seems like it."

Gunny shook his head, picked his ruck off the ground, and heaved it into the LAV-25 light armored vehicle.

The unit was about to move out on a twelve-day training mission in the blistering deserts of Twenty-Nine Palms before deploying to Iraq. Twelve days at The Stumps, as Twenty-Nine Palms is sometimes known, meant twelve days of simulated tactical skirmishes, twelve days of interminable road marches, twelve days of fortifying positions, low crawling, bad food, no showers, and sweltering—that's s-w-e-l-t-e-r-i-n-g—heat.

"You've got a lot to learn, Marine." Gunny ducked into the rear hatch of the LAV.

"What do you mean?" Mitchell called after Gunny.

Gunny climbed back out of the hatch with canteen in hand. "Like don't enter into it, Mitchell. I don't like humping miles across this wasteland, I don't like chiseling foxholes out of this rock-hard desert, I don't like sleeping three hours a night curled up in a poncho, but—"

"But what?"

"But, unlike you, I recognize the whole thing for what it is." He took a swig of water.

"What's that?"

"An opportunity."

"An opportunity for what? The only opportunity I see is an opportunity to sweat and suffer."

Gunny took another hit off his canteen. "You work out, Mitchell?"

"Of course."

"Lift weight?"

"Are you kidding me?" Mitchell proudly flexed his oversized biceps.

"Isn't lifting weight a kind of—what did you call it—punishment?"

"I suppose."

"Feel good?"

Mitchell cocked his head to the right. "Yeah, great," he said with more than a bit of sarcasm, "when I stop."

"If it doesn't feel good, then why do you do it?" Gunny asked. "You like it?"

"I wouldn't say like, but ... heck, Gunny, you know why."

"Yeah, I do." Gunny nodded. "You lift to increase your ability to lift weight—it makes you stronger. To put it another way, it's an opportunity to stretch your capacity to shoulder difficulty."

"Yeah, so?"

"So, that is the very same reason I welcome the so-called punishment *of this exercise."*

"You're not going to give me that old 'that-which-does-not-kill-you-makes-you-stronger' speech, are you?"

"Not exactly, because there's a bit more to it than that," Gunny continues, "If you see the difficulty as just difficulty, it'll be a hard road ahead. But if you can recognize the difficulty for what it is—"

"Pointless torture?" Mitchell interrupted.

Gunny shook his head. "No, like I said before, the difficulty is an opportunity. Difficulty sculpts you in a way that brings out your full potential." Gunny pointed his canteen at Mitchell. "How much stronger would you get in the gym if you lifted no weight."

"I wouldn't get stronger."

"Right. So you need the difficulty that's created by the weight on the barbell to get stronger. Or we could say the difficulty is an opportunity to get stronger."

"Yeah ..."

"The point is this: all difficulties are opportunities for you to increase your capacity for challenge. Rather than trying to avoid the difficulties in life, use them."

"So it's about getting stronger?"

"Yeah, that's a part of it, but it's more than that, too. It's an opportunity to learn what works and what doesn't. It's an opportunity to hone your skills, refine your attitude, and forge a way of being that empowers you—even in the most challenging of circumstances."

Mitchell nodded. "Okay, I can see how you might be on to something."

"I am." Gunny turned to walk away. "Check it out and you'll see."

An opportunity unrecognized is an opportunity wasted. And, unfortunately, a great many of the obstacles we perceive in our lives are really opportunities—unrecognized and wasted. Understanding how to use these opportunities to help stop the vicious cycle of chronic stress is what this lesson, *Drama and Opportunity*, is all about.

In case you haven't been paying attention, life is full of drama: long deployments, relationship difficulties, employment challenges, even traffic and the weather can inject challenge and drama into our lives. And while most of us spend our time trying to get away from such difficulties, in the BOOTSTRAP system these dramas are the places where we train to become more adept at the art of living. Think of each of life's dramas as an opportunity dressed in obstacles' clothing.

As you may have noticed, throughout the BOOTSTRAP process we've placed virtually no focus on controlling our circumstances. As we've learned, struggling against *what's on the screen* is at best a ham-handed approach to stress management, and it's one that usually creates even more suffering and stress than we started with. Instead of wrestling with reality, BOOTSTRAP asks us to modify *our relationship* with reality, to learn how to relax with *what's on the screen* and to thus enjoy a newfound level of peace, ease, and vitality in life. Remember: *Recognize. Release. Restore.*

As you have undoubtedly realized, relaxing with difficult circumstances is often easier said than done. And in many cases it's downright impossible. While this is indisputably true, it's also true that your capacity to relax with difficulty can be increased, and this is one more way that BOOTSTRAP is designed to boost your well-being.

You may have noticed how in the Stress Lab we've been purposely creating mildly difficult and uncomfortable situations with our *recognition sequence*. The idea is to use these challenging circumstances to forge a new way of relating to experience, one marked by relaxation instead of *resistance* and control. It's a method designed to derail the *stress intensifiers* and expand your *circle of serenity*.

The *circle of serenity* is an important concept. It's defined as the imaginary circle of things that you're comfortable with. In other words, in your everyday life you come across all types of situations, events, people, and circumstances, and quite predictably you're able to remain relaxed and serene with some, and just as predictably, others send you for a loop.

Those people, events, and circumstances you are able to easily relax with are said to be *inside* your *circle of serenity;* this means that when you encounter any of these, you are typically able to remain calm, at ease, and serene. On the other hand, all of those things that seem to regularly drive you to frustration or anger are said to be *outside* of your circle. *Inside* the circle: easy to relax with; *outside* the circle: difficult, if not impossible, to relax with. Picture it like this:

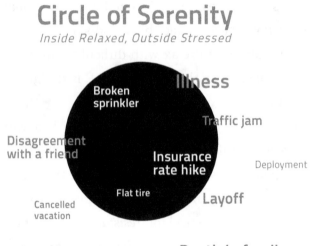

Circle of Serenity
Inside Relaxed, Outside Stressed

Broken sprinkler

Illness

Traffic jam

Disagreement with a friend

Insurance rate hike

Deployment

Flat tire

Cancelled vacation

Layoff

Death in family

We all know people who seem to be ruffled by almost nothing. A layoff? No problem. An IRS audit? Fine. A traffic accident? No biggie. While everyone around them is sent into tailspins, these folks stay calm, cool, and collected no matter what life throws their way. So what is it about these people that makes them so well-equipped to cope artfully with life's challenges? You guessed it: they have an expanded *circle of serenity*. With a larger circle, more things are included, and a great measure of calm and relaxation in life is possible.

This is why, in the BOOTSTRAP process, we seek to fit more things in our *circle of serenity* by expanding it. And our circle is expanded by building our mental and emotional capacity—the capacity to remain undisturbed in more and varied circumstances, especially in situations that have historically thrown us off balance.

Fortunately, building capacity is something that anyone who has been in the military is familiar with, though primarily in the realm of building *physical* capacity. Running to build our cardiovascular capacity and push-ups to build our muscular capacity are just two examples. And while in this case we're interested in increasing our mental and emotional capacity rather than our physical, the process is much the same.

Stress Fact:

An opportunity unrecognized is an opportunity wasted. Most people spend their time trying to get away from difficult and challenging circumstances, completely missing how these situations can actually be beneficial.

Just as a weight lifter needs the challenge of more weight to build their physical capacity; the *stressologist* needs the challenge of difficult life circumstances to build their mental and emotional capacity—that is to say, the capacity to remain relaxed with each moment.

Life's difficulties are opportunities for just this. Use them.

To build physical strength, to increase your capacity to lift weight, you need to lift more weight. Strength builds as you slowly and deliberately lift just a bit more weight than you're comfortable with. If you can easily lift 80 pounds, lift 85; once you can lift 85 without difficulty, move up to 90; and so on. You're *expanding your capacity* for weight lifting by always lifting just a bit more than is comfortable and by staying with the burn.

The same principle applies when you're working to expand your *mental and emotional capacity,* your *circle of serenity.* Here, too, the invitation remains the same: do a bit more than is comfortable and stay with the burn. But for the expansion of our mental and emotional capacity, rather than needing weight to provide the resistance needed for growth, we need difficulty or drama. We need situations and circumstances with which we would normally be unable to relax. This is the *opportunity in the drama.* As for the burn, instead of feeling it in your muscles, you feel it in your emotions; irritation, anger, frustration, impatience are just a few terms to describe the burn that tells us that our *circle of serenity* is being challenged.

To be clear though, if we are truly interested in benefiting from an expanded circle, we need to do more than just encounter difficulty. To expand our circle and thus experience greater ease and happiness in life, we must *consciously relax* in the midst of our *tendency to react* with frustration and anger. It's through the process of deliberately meeting adversity in a new and accepting way that we rewire our nervous systems to remain relaxed and calm no matter *what's on the screen.*

But wait a minute! Why should I be relaxed with difficulty? Shouldn't I attack it, change it, fix it so it will no longer be a problem? For most people, the answer would be a resounding "yes," but those would be the same people who don't understand what we learned way back in lesson one: *what's on the screen* is non-negotiable. It can't be any different from how it is for now, and if we're interested in being relaxed *now*, this approach of control and struggle just won't do.

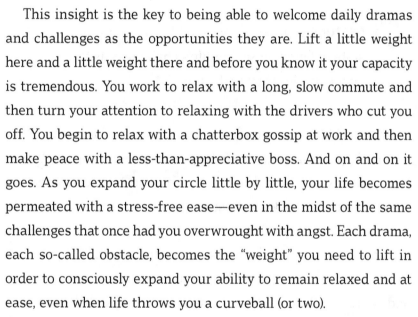

We rewire our nervous systems to remain relaxed and calm no matter what's *on the screen.*

This insight is the key to being able to welcome daily dramas and challenges as the opportunities they are. Lift a little weight here and a little weight there and before you know it your capacity is tremendous. You work to relax with a long, slow commute and then turn your attention to relaxing with the drivers who cut you off. You begin to relax with a chatterbox gossip at work and then make peace with a less-than-appreciative boss. And on and on it goes. As you expand your circle little by little, your life becomes permeated with a stress-free ease—even in the midst of the same challenges that once had you overwrought with angst. Each drama, each so-called obstacle, becomes the "weight" you need to lift in order to consciously expand your ability to remain relaxed and at ease, even when life throws you a curveball (or two).

Once you recognize life's little difficulties as no more an obstacle than the weight on the barbell, you've taken your first step. By appreciating these opportunities dressed in obstacles' clothing and using each one to increase your mental and emotional capacity, you're making a powerful shift in your ability to live peacefully.

Here's how you can apply the three-stage BOOTSTRAP process:

RECOGNIZE the drama as an opportunity to stretch your *circle of serenity.*

RELEASE your tendency to resist the drama/opportunity, and instead *consciously relax* with it as it is. Give it your full permission to be.

RESTORE your body and mind to their natural relaxed state of being by seeing life's challenges as the opportunities they really are.

When you do this over and over with an ever-widening range of dramas/opportunities, your *circle of serenity* expands. Like Gunny Hernandez, you'll have learned to welcome life's challenges as the opportunities they are. Best of all, your capacity to relax with difficulty in your Stress Lab will begin to help you at home, at work, and in all sorts of challenging situations that life throws your way.

But remember, as we mentioned in our last lesson, be realistic and start small. Your *circle of serenity* is expanded when you intentionally challenge yourself to relax with things *barely outside* your comfort zone. It's important to be respectful of your mental and emotional capacity as you begin your efforts here. The idea is to slowly and deliberately increase the intensity of the things you practice with, just like the weight in the gym.

In the same way that you wouldn't attempt to bench press 300 pounds on your first-ever workout, you should also be realistic when lifting the weight of life's dramas. Carelessly working beyond your capacity is likely to cause additional angst and frustration, and there's enough of that to go around already.

Week 5: Stress Lab Experiments™
Recognizing Possibility

1. RECOGNITION SEQUENCE

Download the audio file at www.bootstrapUSA.com/WIP   Enter code: X4LQ8

Use the Recognition Sequence audio recording* to perform the sequence once every other day to conduct the following Stress Lab experiment guided by the four-step N.O.T.E. process: Notice, Observe, Try, and Experience.

> **NOTICE your tendency to treat the dramas and difficulties in your life purely as obstacles.**
>
> Start in your Stress Lab and watch how physical limitations, unmet expectations, and even mental distractions are viewed solely as obstacles to be eliminated.
>
> **OBSERVE how this mindset causes a constant flow of "dram-ortunities" (opportunities to stretch your circle of serenity) to go unnoticed and wasted.**
>
> With your attention placed on what the mind thinks *should be*, examine how you remain distracted from expanding your *circle of serenity* and remain rooted in the cycle of irritation and struggle.
>
> **TRY appreciating and using these dramas and difficulties by consciously relaxing with *what's on the screen*.**
>
> Rewire the way your nervous system reacts to life's ups and downs. Meet disappointing and frustrating situations with a deliberate intention to create a kind of mental and emotional space for them in order to stretch your ability to remain relaxed and expand your *circle of serenity*.
>
> **EXPERIENCE how your ability to remain relaxed grows.**
>
> In the midst of the same circumstances that used to drive you mad, you strangely and unexpectedly find yourself at ease and

unruffled. Your growing *circle of serenity* begins to permeate your life with a sense of peace and happiness.

2. INTENTIONAL RESTORATION

Download the audio file at www.bootstrapUSA.com/WIP   Enter code: X4LQ8

Use the Intentional Restoration audio recording* to perform one session every other day (alternate days with your *recognition sequence* practice).

3. INSTANT INTERVENTIONS

Use as needed throughout your days (see Appendix A).

4. SCIENTIFIC OBSERVATIONS

Spend five minutes at the end of each day using the self-study questions below to make notations in your journal.

– How often do I recognize the dramas and difficulties in my life as opportunities for expanding my *circle of serenity?*

– What effect might a shift toward recognizing the value of obstacles have on my interaction with life's challenges?

– What are some specific obstacles barely outside of my *circle of serenity* that I might begin to practice with? In my Stress Lab? Outside my Stress Lab?

– What is my primary challenge when it comes to expanding my *circle of serenity?*

– How are my BOOTSTRAP practices affecting my stress levels, sense of well-being, emotional state, and relationships with others throughout my day?

How to Enjoy a Thriller
Peaceful Coexistence™

LESSON SUMMARY

- Emotions are a natural and necessary part of the human experience.

- While we can reduce emotional disturbances, it is impossible to eliminate them totally.

- When a challenging emotion is *what's on the screen*, we have no choice but to experience it.

- *Peaceful coexistence,* or relaxing with emotional disturbances, allows us to prevent the creation of unnecessary stress.

Yogic Source
Vairagya
(non-attachment)

How to Enjoy a Thriller
Peaceful Coexistence™

"Don't you give a crap?!" Corporal Johnson screamed at Staff Sergeant Dowling.

Dowling sat quietly in the almost-empty mess hall and looked calmly back at Johnson. He said nothing.

"I'm so pissed I can't even see straight," Johnson said, "and you're just sitting there like nothing happened. We almost got our heads blown off. Don't you get it?"

The two soldiers had just returned from a mission. As members of an explosive ordinance disposal (EOD) unit, every mission was precarious, but last night's had been exceptionally hairy. A roadside bomb had disabled a Stryker infantry carrier vehicle, and a secondary explosive device located adjacent to the initial blast failed to detonate. Dowling and Johnson were called in to detonate the secondary device. It was a fairly routine mission, but one that took a turn for the worse when three snipers opened fire, very nearly putting an end to them both.

Dowling took a sip from his coffee and shook his head. "Look, man," he began in his slow West Texas drawl, "it's not that I don't care. Heck, it's not even that I'm not pissed off."

"No?"

"No. It's just that I've kind of learned to be okay with my anger." He shrugged. "I don't really even feel like I need to act on it. It always passes."

"Whatever, Dowling, but if you ask me, it's not healthy to bottle it up like that."

"That's not it. I'm not bottling or swallowing or suppressing it. It's more like I'm allowing." He cupped his coffee mug in both hands and took another sip, "It's kind of like I've made peace with the fact that the anger is here. It's allowed to come, it's allowed to go. No biggie."

"But it is a biggie." Johnson said a bit more forcefully. "I mean, we almost got our heads blown off!"

"Yeah, I get that. And it pisses me off, too. But back during my first deployment, I learned something."

"Yeah?"

"Yeah. I learned that stirring up my anger with thoughts of revenge and outrage only invites it to stay longer—it makes me feel worse."

"So you stuff it?"

"No, Johnson, you're not listening." Dowling shook his head, "I'm not stuffing it, because that just makes it worse, too. Much worse. In fact, that's a good way to get yourself into real trouble. Being able to live through the stresses of this place requires something in between acting out and suppression. I like to think of it as a kind of peaceful coexistence."

Life is unpredictable. Despite your efforts to ensure that *what's on the screen* will be to your liking, sometimes life simply doesn't cooperate. When going to the theater, even though you do your best to make sure you go to an entertaining movie—you read the reviews, watch the trailers, and get recommendations from friends—sometimes you still end up watching a dud. You're in the mood for *Sleepless in Seattle* and you get *A Nightmare on Elm Street;* although you'd like a light-hearted romantic comedy, you get a thriller.

It's no surprise to find the same thing to be true when it comes to our efforts to manage stress. Despite our best efforts to perform our Stress Lab techniques, complete our experiments, and employ our tools, things don't always turn out as planned. Look to your own experience and you'll see. Although the BOOTSTRAP process has helped you to thwart *resistance,* to rein in *disintegration,* and to expand your *circle of serenity,* even though it's shown you how to conduct experiments, understand the workings of stress, and act as an effective *stressologist,* you still

159

find yourself sometimes getting worked up when things don't go your way. Certain situations, certain memories, certain people still set you off. So what gives?

Well, it's this: you're human. Congratulations.

The truth of the matter is that human beings have emotions. We have thoughts and reactions, and many of them are beyond our control, no matter how much practice we put into training our minds or managing our emotions. Even the Pope and the Dalai Lama have bad days. This means that even though you may be in the mood for a calm, relaxing emotional experience, you may get something altogether different. Instead of a comedy, you get a thriller. Staff Sergeant Dowling recognized this, and so should you.

Stress Fact:

Emotions are a natural and necessary part of life. And this is true even of those so-called negative emotions like anger or grief. The real problem arises when we habitually relate to our emotional experience in a way that intensifies or prolongs its effect.

But what do we do when things aren't going so well? How can we navigate through those times when the messy side of our humanness shows its face, when anger, impatience, or depression is *what's on the screen?* Is there a special BOOTSTRAP technique to help us through that? Fortunately, the answer is "yes." For circumstances that send us quite predictably into a fine fit of frustration, that remain squarely outside of our *circle of serenity*, we have a special technique: *peaceful coexistence.*

Peaceful coexistence is designed for the times when, despite your best efforts, your emotions get the best of you. It's been created to help you through those moments when negative thoughts and emotions are present. The technique recognizes the non-negotiable nature of *what's on the screen*, even when *what's on the screen* is negative thoughts or emotions.

Peaceful coexistence is designed for the times when, despite your best efforts, your emotions get the best of you.

When we're faced with such internal turmoil, whether it's irritation or fear or worry or anger, in that moment you have but three choices: *indulge* the emotion, *resist* the emotion, or *peacefully coexist* with the emotion. And, not surprisingly, each of these will yield a very different result when it comes to your stress and well-being. Let's take a look at each in turn.

Indulgence: To indulge means to oblige, coddle, pamper, or in some manner serve the emotion. It begins with you giving your power over to the emotion and ends with you acting out in the way it's prompting you. Think of Corporal Johnson's outrage. His anger got the better of him, and his tendency is to act on the emotion by expressing his outrage by word or even by deed. This is indulgence.

The trouble with *indulgence* is that when we serve the emotional reaction by acting on it, we inadvertently strengthen the reactive pattern. It's a process that disempowers us and interferes with our ability to remain rational and calm. Think of a spoiled child throwing a tantrum for a piece of candy. Everyone knows that the worst possible thing you can do in that situation is to give the child the piece of candy, to give in to the tantrum. To do so would only reinforce the behavior; the child would learn that by throwing a tantrum, he'll get what he wants. Sure, you've stopped the tantrum for the moment, but by indulging the tantrum—giving in to it—you're also creating a tantrum-throwing monster. You've realized a short-term gain but at a huge long-term cost.

And so it goes with your mind. The emotional reaction you experience as a result of a particular disappointment is your mind's version of the child's tantrum. The tantrum-throwing mind might prompt you into an angry outburst about the stalled line at the supermarket; it could pressure you to snap at the gate agent about a canceled flight; it might urge you to flash the one-finger salute to a slowpoke driver in the fast lane. And just like with the child, when you do what your mind wants, the tantrum stops—the uncomfortable thoughts and emotions subside and you can relax. But stopping the mind's tantrum in this way comes at a cost.

Your long-term cost derives from what you're teaching the mind. By giving in to the emotional reaction, you're teaching the mind that it can get what it wants if it just makes a big enough stink. As a result, you're setting yourself up for an ever-increasing number of mental tantrums, each with the attendant stress, angst, irritation, and despair. And just like the parent of the monstrous tantrum-thrower, you'll soon find yourself doing just about anything to make the ever-increasing tantrums stop. Scream at the kids, honk at the traffic jam, cuss out a friend, all in the name of making the uncomfortable thought or emotion—the mind's tantrum—go away. You'll have become a powerless slave to the tantrum-throwing mind.

So it's easy to see how *indulgence* is a shortsighted strategy and one that in the long run will dramatically increase the incidence of these types of mental and emotional outbursts. And unfortunately, resistance isn't much better.

Resistance: This tendency is in many ways the opposite of *indulgence*. Where indulgence has us acting as the dutiful soldier of the thought or emotion, *resistance* rejects the emotion's very right to exist. The thought "I shouldn't be experiencing this emotion" is at the core of *resistance*, and it's quite common among those engaged in the BOOTSTRAP process. After all, the entire process is about reducing disturbances of mind and emotion. It's therefore only logical to conclude that one's investment of time and energy in this program should put a stop to the parade of negative and unhelpful thoughts and emotions.

Of course, it's true. We've already seen how the BOOTSTRAP process does reduce the incidence of such challenging mental and emotional states. But again, remember that your *circle of serenity* will never include everything in your life, and while we can *reduce* unpleasant, negative emotional reactions, we will never be able to get rid of them altogether.

With that said, let's look back at what we discovered in our third lesson: *resistance is futile.* There we saw the damaging consequences found in resisting an external experience (such as a difficult EOD mission), but the fact is it's just as problematic when we resist an internal experience (such as an emotion). Making matters worse, when we resist our internal experience of an emotional reaction, we end up with two problems instead of one.

If anger arises as a result of a brush with an uncooperative co-worker, I experience anger because anger is part of *what's on the screen.* And when I begin to resist the emotion with the thought "I shouldn't be angry," I unwittingly create a second problem. I'm now saddled with *two* angers instead of one: the first is anger with my co-worker; the second is anger about my anger. My *resistance* has doubled my trouble.

From these examples, it's easy to see how both the habit of *indulgence* and *resistance* lead to less-than-ideal results. Yet despite this, they remain the two primary ways through which most of us unconsciously and automatically deal with our negative mental and emotional states. We do so largely because we remain unaware of the significant negative consequences these habits have on our well-being. This is something you'll get a chance to verify in the Stress Lab this week.

Peaceful Coexistence: Fortunately, the third option doesn't suffer from the same shortcomings. *Peaceful coexistence* is the middle ground between *indulgence* and *resistance.* Rather than catering to the emotion like *indulgence* does or attempting to squash it out of existence like *resistance, peaceful coexistence* recognizes the very first truth outlined in the BOOTSTRAP process: *what's on the screen* is non-negotiable. This means that if anger is present in this moment, if anger is *what's on the screen, peaceful coexistence* realizes that no amount of squirming, whining, conniving, or striving is going to change that fact, at least not in this moment.

> The strategy of *peaceful coexistence* honors the truth that anger is present while recognizing the nature of both negative thought and emotion as naturally-occurring phenomena.

Peaceful coexistence invites you to relax with the disturbance; it means to recognize the feeling as a natural functioning of human life and to allow it to do its thing. If anger arises, your job is to relax and allow the anger to be as it is. The invitation is to *release* any tendency to indulge it with thoughts or actions that empower it, and to *release* any tendency to resist it with thoughts or actions that question its right to be. Another way to say this is that we create a kind of mental space for the anger to exist in—without reacting to its presence.

The strategy of *peaceful coexistence* honors the truth that anger is present while recognizing the nature of both negative thought and emotion as naturally-occurring phenomena. The truth is that anger and, in fact, all emotions are a natural part of the human experience. They arise naturally under certain circumstances and will subside just as naturally if left alone. It's only through *indulgence* and *resistance* that they are able to persist beyond their normal life spans. Remember, while we may be able to reduce the incidence of negative thoughts and emotions, eliminating them totally is simply not possible.

At this point, many will be asking how it could be possible to relax in the presence of anger, for isn't relaxation the opposite of anger? And the same could be asked about worry, frustration, fear, and anxiety. Yet another fair question.

First off, it will help to recognize anger for what it is. Anger is not anger so much as it is a pattern of bodily sensations. When anger arises, if you look at the experience without naming it, you'll see that it is simply tightness in the chest, heaviness in the belly, pressure in the throat. Check it out for yourself and you'll see

Remember that your *circle of serenity* will never include everything in your life, and while we can reduce unpleasant, negative emotional reactions, we will never be able to get rid of them altogether.

that whenever anger arises, you're experiencing a surprisingly similar pattern of physical sensations no matter what it was that triggered your anger.

The same is true for all emotions. They are experienced as simple patterns of sensation in the body. Anger is one pattern, sadness another, and worry yet another. When you recognize this, you're then poised to relax, not with the idea of the emotion but with the sensation. Relax with the simple pattern of tightness-heaviness-pressure. Can you relax with anger? No way. Can you relax with this simple pattern of sensations? You'll be surprised.

This ability to experience thoughts and emotions in a new way can greatly enhance our ability to peacefully coexist with emotional disturbances.

Try this: next time you're experiencing a bothersome emotion, close your eyes, take a deep breath, and relax. Now bring your attention to the *experience* of the emotion—that is, the sensations or the *felt sense* of the experience in the body. Identify its size, its shape, its location, and its intensity. The intention here is to feel the experience of what you would typically label as sadness or anger or worry or whatever the emotion may be and to do so free from the label and its usual associations.

Once you have a sense of the size, shape, location, and intensity (again, free from the label), ask yourself, "Can I relax with this?" If someone offered you $1,000, could you relax with it for three minutes? If the answer is "yes," then why not now? And if you could relax with it for three minutes, why not thirty? Your task here is to explore the possibility of peacefully coexisting with the sensations we typically call sadness or anger or worry. Seek to relax not with the *emotion* but with the *sensations* that make up the emotion.

You'll find that when approached in this way, it's easier than you might think, for great sadness is really just tightness here and heaviness there. Anxiety is simply tingling here and gripping there. The same can be said for each and every emotion we could possibly experience.

It's important also to keep in mind that when I say relax with, the key word is not *relax* but *with*. It's a critical distinction because in our endeavor to *relax with* a disturbance, our natural tendency is to try to relax *instead* of experiencing the disturbance. We attempt to relax *instead* of being sad, *instead* of being angry, *instead* of being disturbed. And this is not the idea at all.

Relaxing with means relaxing right alongside of anger without needing it to change or dissolve in any form or fashion. *Relaxing with* means to relax in the midst of great sadness without wishing for it to subside. *Relaxing with* means to relax in the presence of worry without scheming for its demise. And again, to be successful in this, it helps greatly to experience the emotion not as emotion but as a felt pattern of sensations. Just feel it, without the labels, associations, and stories we all typically apply to a particular emotional state. Just feel.

Here's how you can apply the three-stage BOOTSTRAP process:

RECOGNIZE your tendency to react to disturbing emotions with *indulgence* or *resistance*. Notice how it makes your experience worse.

RELEASE your habit of reacting and instead *relax with*, or *peacefully coexist* with, the emotion.

RESTORE your body's ability to flow with the natural rhythms of thought and emotion while hastening your return to the natural relaxed state.

This is what we'll be up to in the Stress Lab this week. But remember, just as you wouldn't expect to have success skiing down the most advanced run on the slopes your first time out, it's important to keep in mind that at first your capacity to *relax with* so-called negative emotions will be modest. So don't start with emotions spawned by a heated argument with a spouse but instead begin with the mild impatience that arises as a result of a slow line at the grocery store or the moderate irritation of a spilled cup of coffee. As with all endeavors in life, we must respect our capacity, start small, and work our way toward greater accomplishments.

Master this technique of *peaceful coexistence*, of *relaxing with*, and you'll be well poised to remain calm and at ease with whatever is *on the screen* of your life—even if at times it does seem more like *A Nightmare on Elm Street* than you'd like.

Week 6: Stress Lab Experiments™
Peaceful Coexistence™

1. RECOGNITION SEQUENCE

*Download the audio file at www.bootstrapUSA.com/WIP   Enter code: X4LQ8

Use the Recognition Sequence audio recording* to perform the sequence once every other day to conduct the following Stress Lab experiment guided by the four-step N.O.T.E. process: Notice, Observe, Try, and Experience.

NOTICE your strong and immediate tendency to either indulge or resist negative emotions.

In your *recognition sequence* and in life, watch how you tend to immediately react to emotional experiences with either *indulgence* or *resistance*. Be curious about what your particular habit is: do you resist most often, or indulge? No judgment, just notice.

OBSERVE how both indulging and resisting emotions have the effect of intensifying and prolonging the emotional disturbance.

Study the effects of both your *indulgence* and your *resistance* of emotions in your own experience. Feel how these habits can fuel the emotion. Examine how your involvement with the emotion (through either *indulgence* or *resistance)* invites it to stay.

TRY *relaxing with* emotions by experiencing them without the usual labels and associations. *Peacefully coexist* with them.

Make no effort to get rid of the emotion. Instead focus on feeling the unlabeled sensations that make up the emotion. With your attention focused on the raw sensations, simply relax right alongside them. Give them your permission to be there. Breathe.

EXPERIENCE how you're able to remain relaxed in the midst of the same emotions that once tormented you.

When experienced free from the labels and ideas we have about an emotion, we're more able to relax because the experience isn't judged as bad or wrong. It just is.

2. INTENTIONAL RESTORATION

*Download the audio file at www.bootstrapUSA.com/WIP   Enter code: X4LQ8

Use the Intentional Restoration audio recording* to perform one session every other day (alternate days with your *recognition sequence* practice).

3. INSTANT INTERVENTIONS

Use as needed throughout your days (see Appendix A).

4. SCIENTIFIC OBSERVATIONS

Spend five minutes at the end of each day using the self-study questions below to make notations in your journal.

– When it comes to unwanted mental and emotional states, what is my tendency? To *indulge, resist,* or *peacefully coexist?*

– How does my habitual reaction to unwanted mental and emotional states help or hinder my stress levels?

– Have I ever really experienced emotions free from their labels?

– How might cultivating the ability to experience emotion as pure sensation contribute to my ability to *relax with,* or *peacefully coexist* with, my emotions?

– How does *peaceful coexistence* change my experience of my emotions?

– How are my BOOTSTRAP practices affecting my stress levels, sense of well-being, emotional state, and relationships with others throughout my day?

The Tranquil Moviegoer™
Effort and Acceptance:
the Balanced Approach

LESSON SUMMARY

In the BOOTSTRAP system:

- *Effort* refers to your work to create greater peace in your life.

- *Acceptance* refers to your commitment to relax with however the results of your efforts turn out.

Combining *effort* and *acceptance* in equal measure is the formula for maximum benefit.

Yogic Source
Abhyasa & Vairagya
(practice & non-attachment)

The Tranquil Moviegoer
Effort and Acceptance: the Balanced Approach

"Damn it!" Sergeant David Kirkpatrick slammed the spoon to the table. Blood-red tomato soup splattered across the surface of the gleaming white linoleum.

Holly Milford, Kirkpatrick's occupational therapist, calmly wiped up the soup and then looked up to her patient.

"David," she said in her always-calm tone, "you okay?"

Kirkpatrick nodded. "Yeah, sorry. It's just so frustrating." The word frustrating landed hard.

"I know it is," Holly said.

With several months of therapy already under his belt, Kirkpatrick is still having difficulty with many everyday tasks—like eating soup with a spoon.

Earlier in the year, his deployment in Afghanistan was cut short when a Taliban improvised explosive device (IED) tore through the Humvee he was riding in. Though lucky to escape the ordeal with his life, his shoulder caught the worst of the blast, leaving him with nerve damage in his right arm and shoulder.

"It's just that I should be able to do this by now!" Kirkpatrick picked the spoon up with renewed vigor and again tried to navigate a few ounces of soup from the bowl to his mouth. The expression on his face: one part frustration, three parts determination. But most of the soup again ended up on the already-soup-stained bib rather than in his mouth.

"Jeez!" Again the spoon met the table hard.

Milford placed her reassuring hand on Kirkpatrick's arm. "Okay, let's take a minute." She again wiped the table.

Kirkpatrick's breath was labored under his irritation.

"Do me a favor, David." She leaned forward and looked him in the eyes, "Close your eyes and let's take a couple of deep breaths together."

"Like that's going to help my arm?"

"Just play along, huh?" She smiled.

"Fair enough." Kirkpatrick closed his eyes and sighed.

"Good." Holly squeezed his arm. "Now follow my rhythm. Breathe in. Breathe out."

She continued for a few moments. "With each exhalation, r-e-l-a-x," she coached.

The air of frustration around Kirkpatrick softened.

"Very good. Now open your eyes slowly."

Kirkpatrick seemed a new man.

"Better?" Holly smiled.

"Yeah."

"Okay, so here's the deal. We're going to maintain this relaxed state and try it again. But maintaining a relaxed state is much more important than getting that confounded spoon into your mouth. That soup's terrible anyway," she chided.

Kirkpatrick nodded.

"Remember, it's about relaxing, not achieving."

"Got it." Kirkpatrick took a deep breath and let it out with a relaxed sigh. He took the spoon in his hand and slowly dipped it into the soup. His arm moved slowly. Each time he tensed, he paused, breathed, and relaxed before proceeding. The spoon made it to his mouth with almost no spillage.

Holly grinned. "How about that?"

Kirkpatrick looked astounded. "How did that happen?"

"It's your impatience."

"Huh?"

"I know you're well intentioned, but your impatience is causing internal conflict—and that's interfering with your coordination."

"I just want to get it right." He motioned to his soup-covered bib. "I don't look so good in bibs."

"I get it." Holly nodded. "I know how sincere you are, but here's the thing: believe it or not, our enthusiasm for progress can actually interfere with our progress."

"I thought enthusiasm is good."

"In general it is, but sometimes it can backfire when our enthusiasm leads to self-criticism and frustration."

Kirkpatrick nodded.

"It's a balance: one part effort and one part acceptance. That's the key."

Holly has recognized one of the primary stumbling blocks in our quest to rid ourselves of chronic of stress. It's a pitfall that regularly trips up practitioners of the BOOTSTRAP process and, ironically, it's most pronounced in those who are the most committed and enthusiastic about their success. The problem is that without a *balanced approach*, the very efforts designed to rid ourselves of stress can actually become the source of more stress in our lives.

Let's say I'm stressed about my job responsibilities. I start working on my stress and then begin to get stressed out about reducing my stress. I wonder if I'm doing the techniques right. I criticize myself for the days when I don't do my experiments wholeheartedly. I constantly judge my performance. I worry that I'll never be free of the demoralizing effects of stress. In short, I'm getting worse! It's a catch-22 in which my enthusiasm for progress actually gets in the way of my progress.

To counter this, it's important to approach the techniques—

and all our efforts to rid ourselves of chronic stress—with two seemingly contradictory concepts in mind. They are ideas that have been borrowed from one of yoga's most ancient and important source texts, and when used together, they neatly interrupt this self-defeating habit. These dueling intentions are *effort* and *acceptance*.

Effort, in our case, refers to our work to quiet the mind, to disentangle from emotions, and to relieve stress by creating a greater sense of ease and joy in our lives. Here, of course, we accomplish this through the BOOTSTRAP techniques we've been working with all along: the *recognition sequence*, *intentional restoration*, daily experiments, and the rest of our tools. By now, through your participation in the BOOTSTRAP process, your *effort* is likely well-established.

> *Acceptance* means to remain at ease with how the techniques and our stress levels are evolving.

Acceptance, however, may be another matter, for this idea may seem a little out of place at first. *Acceptance* refers to our ability to remain at ease with how the techniques—and our stress levels— are evolving. What this means is that we must do our techniques, devote ourselves to the experiments, but at the same time accept our progress *as it is*. To use the language of the BOOTSTRAP process, we perform the technique and *relax with* the results we

Stress Fact:

The *balanced approach* blends *effort* and *acceptance* in equal measure.

Effort without *acceptance* yields a situation in which frustration and stress are created through the very means we use to rid ourselves of frustration and stress.

Acceptance without *effort* yields a situation in which the cycle of chronic stress is allowed to continue.

The *balanced approach* interrupts chronic stress in the most effective manner.

get. After all, the results we get are *what's on the screen,* and we've already seen the dire consequences of arguing with that.

Together these two concepts help us create what we call a *balanced approach:* one part *effort,* one part *acceptance.* It means cultivating both discipline and trust within our work: the discipline to perform the techniques regularly and with full effort and a trust in their effectiveness. When working the BOOTSTRAP program, the *balanced approach* looks like this: each day you remain committed to your daily Stress Lab experiments, you do your *recognition sequence* and you use your *instant interventions* to interrupt the cycle of stress throughout your day. In other words, you do your part. When your stress levels are low, you relax and accept how your efforts are paying off; when your stress levels flare up, ushering anger or frustration into your life, you relax and accept how your efforts are paying off. No matter the results, you do your part and accept what you get.

By using *effort* and *acceptance* side by side, you'll find new power and ease in the process. But remember, when the results aren't what your mind might think they should be (and this is important), don't give up, doubt the effectiveness of the techniques, or self-judge. Continue with the process: *effort* and *acceptance* together at the same time—all along the way.

Here's how you can apply the three-stage BOOTSTRAP process:

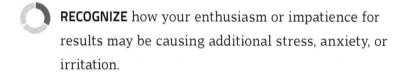 **RECOGNIZE** how your enthusiasm or impatience for results may be causing additional stress, anxiety, or irritation.

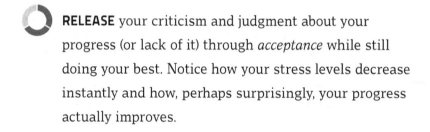 **RELEASE** your criticism and judgment about your progress (or lack of it) through *acceptance* while still doing your best. Notice how your stress levels decrease instantly and how, perhaps surprisingly, your progress actually improves.

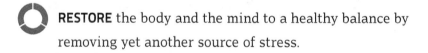 **RESTORE** the body and the mind to a healthy balance by removing yet another source of stress.

Week 7: Stress Lab Experiments™
Effort and Acceptance: the Balanced Approach

1. RECOGNITION SEQUENCE
Download the audio file at www.bootstrapUSA.com/WIP   Enter code: X4LQ8

Use the Recognition Sequence audio recording* to perform the sequence once every other day to conduct the following Stress Lab experiment guided by the four-step N.O.T.E. process: Notice, Observe, Try, and Experience.

> **NOTICE your tendency to judge and criticize yourself or the process when the BOOTSTRAP techniques seem to be working less effectively than you think they should.**
>
> Everyone has good days and bad, and you'll notice that the same is true as you use your BOOTSTRAP techniques. This means that some days you'll welcome your *recognition sequence* and other days you'll hate it. Some days you'll find that your stress levels are managed and relaxed and other days you'll wonder if any of your techniques are working at all. Know that this is the normal functioning of the process.
>
> **OBSERVE how your criticisms of your progress increase your stress levels beyond where they were.**
>
> Watch how your judgments affect your well-being and your continued engagement in the BOOTSTRAP process. Nothing can derail your stress-management progress faster than the critical mind. Getting stressed about stress management is not what it's all about.   -
>
> **TRY accepting the results as they come to you, positive together with negative.**
>
> No matter how your Stress Lab experiments are working, no matter how your day unfolds, no matter what your stress levels are, continue with your balanced BOOTSTRAP approach. It's one part *effort*, one part *acceptance* working together all along the way.

EXPERIENCE how yet another source of stress has been eliminated from your life.

Once you accept how the process is working for you and you've let go of the judgment about your progress, that's one less thing to get worked up about. And because you're investing the required *effort* into the process, you can relax knowing that the process is working on both body and mind. The payoff is coming. Trust in the process.

2. INTENTIONAL RESTORATION

*Download the audio file at www.bootstrapUSA.com/WIP   Enter code: X4LQ8

Use the Intentional Restoration audio recording* to perform one session every other day (alternate days with your *recognition sequence* practice).

3. INSTANT INTERVENTIONS

Use as needed throughout your days (see Appendix A).

4. SCIENTIFIC OBSERVATIONS

Spend five minutes at the end of each day using the self-study questions below to make notations in your journal.

– In what ways does my enthusiasm for progress toward eliminating my stress actually cause me stress?

– Can I cultivate a *balanced approach* to my health and well-being? Equal parts *effort* and *acceptance?*

– When I'm not accepting of my progress, how do I feel? Does it do anything to improve my situation?

– How often do I forget that my own mental and emotional reactions are part of *what's on the screen?*

– How are my BOOTSTRAP practices affecting my stress levels, sense of well-being, emotional state, and relationships with others throughout my day?

Onward
Maintaining a Healthy Balance

LESSON SUMMARY

- A tool must be used if it is to have any value to you.
  The tools of the BOOTSTRAP system are no different.

- Even after your initial seven-week program, it's best to
  remain connected to the process.

- Monitor your stress levels, and use the BOOTSTRAP
  tools as often as feels appropriate for you.

Yogic Source
Svadhyaya
(self study)

Onward!

Maintaining a Healthy Balance

Congratulations! You're now armed and ready to manage the process through which stress arises and in a way that few others can. Over the past several weeks, you've learned how the overstimulation of the body's natural stress response can set us up for a whole range of harmful and crippling conditions. You've discovered how the *conditions of perpetuation* lead to a chronic stimulation of our *fight-or-flight response*. And you've seen how this chronic stimulation interferes with the body's ability to rejuvenate itself via a return to its normal relaxed state. Further, you've witnessed first-hand how the *stress intensifiers* of *resistance* and *disintegration* can tighten and prolong the hold that chronic stress has on us, and how our habitual efforts to escape stress and discomfort can actually create more of the same. Finally, you've practiced some powerful techniques to interrupt the out-of-control spiral of chronic stress, including *conscious feeling* and *peaceful coexistence*, techniques that you've hopefully been able to use both in your Stress Lab experiments and in your everyday life.

With all this accomplished, it's important to understand that the work is not done. While you've been armed with an uncommon level of understanding about the workings of stress, and you've been given some extraordinarily powerful tools to combat its presence, the fact remains that these tools, like any tools, must be used if they are to do you any good. In the same way that $3,000 worth of tools from Home Depot won't build you a house unless you take them out of the tool chest, your BOOTSTRAP tools will do nothing for your stress unless you practice them regularly and with sincerity.

Stress Fact:

The BOOTSTRAP system has been proven effective in managing chronic stress over the long term.

Although it may not be necessary for you to practice with the same intensity you have over the past seven weeks, it will nevertheless serve you to maintain a regular connection with these ideas and techniques. You see, the cycle of chronic stress comes from habits that may, for the moment, be interrupted, but we must remember that most of us are working against twenty, thirty, or more years of ingrained habits. These habits can, and probably will, come back the first time it looks as if the coast is clear. I say this from my own experience.

I've studied and practiced these ancient teachings intensely for nearly two decades, yet when I abandon my regular practice, I notice that a battalion of self-sabotaging habits and tendencies from days past comes charging back into my life. And as a result, I find that my quality of life reverts back to its once-dissatisfying state. I've seen the same thing happen with my students as well.

So while an apple a day keeps the doctor away, a similar thing can be said for our practices here: "throw your BOOTSTRAP practices away and your chronic stress is likely to come back and clobber you upside the head." Not as catchy as the apple rhyme, I know, but I never claimed to be a poet.

So as you move forward, I recommend that you keep an eye on how you feel, monitor your stress levels, and use your BOOTSTRAP tools appropriately. If your stress levels are still on the high side and are negatively affecting your energy levels and overall sense of well-being, it's probably a good idea to continue at this pace. However, if much of your stress has abated, it's okay to notch things back a bit and practice the techniques only three or four times a week.

The key here is that you continue to pay attention to how you feel, and when stress levels increase, increase your use of the techniques; when stress levels decrease, you can back off a little. It's recommended, however, that you always maintain a base-level practice of a few times a week to enable the body to fully recover from life's challenges. And you can help further by creating space in your life for relaxation, ample sleep, and proper nutrition.

Onward: Stress Lab Experiments
Maintaining a Healthy Balance

1. RECOGNITION SEQUENCE
Download the audio file at www.bootstrapUSA.com/WIP   Enter code: X4LQ8

Use the Recognition Sequence audio recording* to perform the sequence as needed to conduct the following Stress Lab experiment guided by the four-step N.O.T.E. process. Recommended minimum practice is three times per week:

> **NOTICE how your stress levels naturally rise and fall with different situations and circumstances.**
>
> Remember, stress is a natural part of being human. Only when it gets significantly out of balance does it becomes a problem. With this in mind, create a habit of monitoring your stress, both when it's low and when it rises. This way you'll be ready to use your BOOTSTRAP techniques before stress levels get out of control.
>
> **OBSERVE the connection between your stress levels and your use of the BOOTSTRAP techniques.**
>
> If you stop practicing the *recognition sequence* for a few days, for example, watch how your ability to handle difficult situations changes. Likewise, when you're regularly using the techniques, appreciate how you're able to maintain a more relaxed state of being.
>
> **TRY applying the BOOTSTRAP techniques to a lesser or greater degree in response to your stress levels.**
>
> The BOOTSTRAP process is about stress management, not simply stress relief. That means the techniques give you the power to actively manage your stress levels, but to do this, of course, you must be willing to apply the tools as needed.
>
> **EXPERIENCE how the skillful application of the BOOTSTRAP tools enables you to successfully manage stress as it shows up in your daily life.**

Your regular use of the concepts and techniques you have learned will empower you to consistently manage your stress for years to come. Best of all, the more regularly you use the tools, the better you'll get and the better you'll feel.

2. INTENTIONAL RESTORATION

Download the audio file at www.bootstrapUSA.com/WIP   Enter code: X4LQ8

Use the Intentional Restoration audio recording* to perform sessions as needed.

3. INSTANT INTERVENTIONS

Use as needed throughout your days (see Appendix A).

4. SCIENTIFIC OBSERVATIONS

Spend five minutes at the end of each day using the self-study questions below to make notations in your journal.

- What form does stress typically take in my body? Tightness in the chest, shallowness of breathing, heaviness in the belly?

- What effect do prolonged episodes of intensified stress have on my mental and physical well-being? On my relationships? On my work life?

- In what ways am I contributing to my stress?

- Do I allow stress levels to build to unreasonably high levels before actively using my BOOTSTRAP techniques?

- How are my BOOTSTRAP practices affecting my stress levels, sense of well-being, emotional state, and relationships with others throughout my day?

- What effect might a measured and regular practice of the BOOTSTRAP techniques have on my life?

AFTERWARD

Since 2009, when we first conducted the trials for the BOOTSTRAP yoga program, we've been able to serve over 5,000 U.S. military service members and veterans. From the beginning, our goal has been to provide an effective means for the many thousands struggling with service-related stress imbalances who, for reasons of geography, bureaucracy, or simply a reluctance to enter the mental health system, are not getting the help they need.

Although, I'll admit to being overjoyed with the success of the program thus far, our work is far from done. According to the U.S. Department of Veterans Affairs, of the 2.7 million service members and veterans who deployed to Iraq or Afghanistan, up to 20% have full-blown post-traumatic stress. That's over 500,000 of our sons and daughters; too many of whom have yet to get the help they need. It's for this reason that our work to assist our returning warriors continues, although it's not all we strive for.

Over the past few years, we've increasingly seen the

BOOTSTRAP program being used for more than stress management. We've received emails and letters from troops and veterans all around the globe who are using BOOTSTRAP's wisdom and techniques to live happier lives independent of their stress levels.

The fact is that we can all benefit from becoming more skilled at managing our internal lives. Thoughts, emotions, moods, and habits of mind play such a central role in our happiness and well-being, it only makes sense to consciously and deliberately manage them. And of course this is as true for civilians as it is for our military members.

It's for this reason that we are expanding our focus to bring BOOTSTRAP, in various forms, to help people from all walks of life. From schools to workplaces, and from prisons to hospitals, our goal is to create a movement of millions upon millions who are becoming ever more skilled in managing their humanness—and living more joyfully as a result. This book is but one of our first steps.

If you too believe that a world populated with happier, healthier people can't help but benefit us all, we humbly ask for your support: please spread the word about BOOTSTRAP's free help for troops and veterans and pass this book along to someone you know who could use a little boost.

A Final Thank You

It is my fervent hope that Waging Inner Peace and the BOOTSTRAP system have been in some small way helpful to you. As you might imagine, we'd love to hear how the program and the techniques it contains have benefitted you. So please stay in touch.

Also, if you or someone you know is involved with a company or organization who may wish to employ some variation of the BOOTSTRAP system, do give us a shout. We're always eager to work with partners to bring more lightness, ease, and productivity into people's lives.

Finally, to stay up to date on the latest happenings regarding BOOTSTRAP and my other projects, including events, workshops, instructor trainings and more, join our mailing list at my website below.

To your greatest happiness,

E

www.EricWal.com

BOOTSTRAP®

APPENDICES

APPENDIX A

Technique Addendum

As we've already seen in the BOOTSTRAP Techniques section, five techniques are central to the BOOTSTRAP system. They are:

- Recognition Sequence
- Intentional Restoration
- Instant Interventions
- Scientific Observation
- Personal Commitment

This section is designed to help you learn about the *instant intervention* techniques and to show you how to use them to help derail stress throughout your day. In addition, at the end of this section you will find photographs of all the postures in the *recognition sequence* to help you better understand how to perform the sequence.

For additional guidance on how to get the very most out of your BOOTSTRAP practices, learning videos are available at **www.bootstrapUSA.com/WIP**.

Instant Interventions™

Instant interventions are tools central to the BOOTSTRAP process and tools that differ from most other aspects of the program in two important ways: they're designed to be *targeted*, and they're meant to be *portable*.

Targeted means the techniques are intended to be employed to counteract a specific situation that has triggered your stress and knocked you off balance. The *instant interventions* have been created to help you break the sequence of thoughts that perpetuate your stress response during a *specific episode* of increased anxiety. It might help to think of the other tools of the BOOTSTRAP process as a kind of multivitamin—used to promote overall health and well-being, and the *instant interventions* as more like an aspirin that serves to combat a particular incident of discomfort.

Portable means these techniques are suitable for use wherever you are. Unlike the BOOTSTRAP techniques designed to be performed in your home Stress Lab, the *instant interventions* can be used whether you're at home, at work, deployed or simply out for a walk with your dog. These techniques have been crafted to efficiently and effectively interrupt the thoughts that perpetuate stress, anywhere, any time.

Each of the four *instant intervention* techniques asks that you perform a simple task with your full attention focused on the direct experience of the task. Each intervention works by directing attention away from disturbing and stress-producing thoughts, thereby robbing the cycle of stress of the fuel it needs for its continued existence. Because they rely on your focused attention, for the interventions to be effective you must concentrate sincerely and wholeheartedly. Withdraw attention from thoughts and direct attention to the performance of the technique. When attention becomes distracted, immediately returning to the technique will help lessen the cycle of stress.

The Four Instant Interventions are:

- Heartfelt Gratitude

- Focused Walking

- Victorious Breathing

- Conscious Sipping

HEARTFELT GRATITUDE - This intervention involves intentionally re-creating a feeling of gratitude, love, or appreciation for someone or something in your life. One part visualization and one part concentration, it has the power to effectively interrupt stress patterns and alter the state of the nervous system. Here's the technique:

1. Close your eyes and visualize or imagine a person, place, or thing that brings a sense of love, gratitude, or happiness into your life.

2. Direct your attention to feel the space around your heart. Imagine a chamber there, filling with each inhalation, softening with each exhalation.

3. Combine the feeling of love, gratitude, or happiness with the softness felt around the chamber around the heart.

4. Continue to sense expansion around the heart as you breathe in and sense the softening around the heart as you breathe out, all the while cultivating the feeling of gratitude or happiness.

5. Continue for a minimum of three minutes.

FOCUSED WALKING - Although most of us spend quite a bit of time walking in our daily lives, few of us do so consciously and mindfully. *Focused walking* asks us to focus attention on counting backward from twenty as we walk at a brisk pace. It works like this:

1. Start a brisk walk in a safe area, away from traffic and other distractions.

2. Each time your left foot hits the ground, count down one more number from twenty until you get to zero. At zero, begin again at twenty.

3. If you lose count at any time, restart the count at twenty.

4. Maintain 100% of your concentration on the backward counting throughout your walk.

5. Walk this way for a minimum of five minutes.

VICTORIOUS BREATHING - This is a special technique in which the breath is made audible by a slight narrowing at the back of the throat. The combination of a measured breath together with focused attention creates a powerful effect.

1. Sit in a comfortable position, upright with an erect spine.
2. Close your eyes and bring your attention to the current rhythm of the breath.
3. Breathe only through the nose as you slightly contract the muscles at the back of the throat so that the breath becomes audible (it should sound like a gentle hissing as the breath moves in and out).*
4. Consciously slow and lengthen the breath by using fuller-than-normal inhalations and exhalations. Do not allow the breath to become forceful or harsh.
5. Keep attention trained on the sound and the feeling of the breath as it moves past the contraction at the back of the throat. Continue with long, smooth, easy breaths again only through the nose.
6. Breathe this way for three minutes.

If you feel breath starved at any time, simply relax and return to your normal breath. Resume the technique when you are comfortable.

If you have difficulty creating the back-of-the-throat contraction and gentle hissing sound, think of the way you hold the throat when fogging a mirror with your breath. Victorious breathing uses the same technique, but all breathing is done through the nose, with the mouth closed.

CONSCIOUS SIPPING - Bringing full attention to all the details of slowly drinking a cold beverage is at the heart of *conscious sipping*. My beverage of choice for this exercise is orange juice because of its taste, coldness, and consistency, but any flavored beverage will do (though chilled drinks work best). It works like this:

1. Pour a small amount of a beverage into a glass. Typically, half a glass will be more than sufficient.

2. Sit comfortably, upright with an erect spine.

3. Close your eyes and take a few deep, smooth breaths; relax more with each exhalation.

4. Keeping your eyes closed, bring the glass slowly to your mouth. Feel the hardness of the glass, its temperature, and its shape as it touches your lips. Slowly tilt the glass to drink your beverage. Feel the temperature and wetness of the beverage. Sip in only an ounce or two of liquid. As you do, feel the temperature of the liquid on your lips, in your mouth, on your tongue. Notice the details of the flavor and the response of your mouth. As you swallow, follow the sensations of coolness as the liquid moves down your throat. Be fully engaged with every detail.

5. Repeat until the beverage is gone or the stress episode has been broken.

Remember: Experiment with the various techniques and use the one that works best for you. But no matter which intervention you use, the power of your concentration is what makes the technique effective in interrupting the cycle of stress. Simply doing the techniques, without the intense focus on the experience, will not measurably affect your stress levels. Be intensely engaged.

Recognition Sequence™
Posture Quick Reference Guide

We've already seen how proper performance of the *recognition sequence* is crucial for your success with the BOOTSTRAP system. For this reason we've created a number of resources to help you master the sequence. On the pages that follow is a listing of the postures together with photographs to assist you to do just this.

Remember too, you can obtain our learning videos with more detailed information including the full *recognition sequence video* and a *video posture guide* at **www.bootstrapUSA.com/WIP**

Warm Up Flow

Lunge

Forward Fold

Plank

Downward Dog

Side Bend

Warrior

Reverse Warrior

Side Angle

Chair Pose

Standing Hand to Foot

Shoulder Opener

Cobra

Locust

Childs

Bound Angle

Seated Twist

Knees to Chest

Reclined Twist

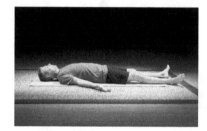

Relaxation

For more detailed information regarding the performance of the postures, together with detailed alignment guidance, please see the *recognition sequence video* and *video posture guide* downloads and DVDs.

Available at:

www.bootstrapUSA.com/WIP

APPENDIX B
BOOTSTRAP® Glossary

Balanced Approach – The most effective method for engaging in the BOOTSTRAP system. One part effort and one part acceptance, the *balanced approach* allows you to do your best while remaining relaxed throughout the process. (see Week 7)

Chronic Stress – A stress condition in which the *stress response* has become persistently activated in a way that doesn't allow the nervous system to return to its normal relaxed state. (see Stress: Friend or Foe)

Circle of Serenity – The circle of things with which one can remain undisturbed and at ease. Situations and circumstances that are outside one's circle will predictably result in frustration, anger, or irritation. The BOOTSTRAP system seeks to expand the *circle of serenity* so that more and more life situations are easeful. (see Week 5)

Commitment – One of the five BOOTSTRAP techniques inviting participants to commit fully to the process. *Commitment* is the energy that fuels the process. (see BOOTSTRAP Overview)

Condition of Perpetuation – Any one of two conditions, each of which can prolong the activation of the *stress response*. The conditions are:

frozen stress response and *misperception of threat*. (see Stress: Friend or Foe)

Conscious Feeling – The practice of directing attention away from thoughts and onto physical sensations in the body. The technique interrupts the internal process through which stress can be intensified. (see Week 4)

Disintegration – the state in which attention is divided among various competing elements of experience. Different thoughts, sights, and sounds fragment attention, creating a sense of overwhelm or stress. The opposite of *integration*. (see Week 3)

Equation of Suffering – This equation describes the manner in which resistance to *what's on the screen* creates suffering. The equation is: Experience + Resistance = Suffering. See also *resistance* and *suffering*. (see Week 2)

Fight-or-flight response (also fight, flight, freeze response) – A condition created by the *sympathetic nervous system* to respond to a real or perceived threat. Involving the releases of stress hormones into the blood stream (epinephrine, norepinephrine, and cortisol primarily), the *fight-or-flight response* prompts the body and mind into a state of heightened readiness. (see Stress: Friend or Foe)

Instant Intervention – One of the five BOOTSTRAP techniques, *instant interventions* are four portable techniques designed to interrupt specific episodes of unnecessary stress. (see Appendix A)

Integration – The state in which attention is fully focused on the task at hand. Sometimes referred to as being "in the zone" by athletes, *integration* creates a sense of calm, focus, and fulfillment. See also *disintegration*. (see Week 3 & 4)

Intentional Restoration – One of the five BOOTSTRAP techniques. Similar to a type of guided relaxation, *intentional restoration* is related to an ancient yogic technique called yoga nidra. Performed lying down, the technique works to reset the nervous system to its relaxed and balanced state. (see BOOTSTRAP Techniques)

N.O.T.E. process – A four-step process at the heart of the daily techniques performed in the Stress Lab. The process is designed to stimulate understanding through personal experimentation and experience. The four steps are: *notice, observe, try, and experience.* (see Weekly Stress Lab Experiments)

Pain – Refers to the discomfort caused by the simple experience of the moment, prior to labels, judgment, or analysis. Distinct from suffering, pain that is arising in any given moment is mandatory. See also *suffering.* (see Week 2)

Peaceful Coexistence – The technique of relaxing with disturbances that cannot be changed. These disturbances can be external, such as a work situation, or internal, like a thought or emotion. (see Week 6)

Recognition Sequence – One of the five BOOTSTRAP techniques involving a series of physical postures or exercises. Though the sequence appears to be physical in nature, it is actually designed to accomplish two primary objectives: interrupt the cycle of chronic stress; illuminate the ways in which chronic stress is unconsciously fueled. (see BOOTSTRAP Techniques)

Recognize – The first step in the three-step BOOTSTRAP system. *Recognize* refers to the act of consciously noticing the mental habits and tendencies that fuel chronic stress. (see BOOTSTRAP Process)

Release – The second step in the three-step BOOTSTRAP system. *Release* refers to the act of intentionally releasing participation in habits and tendencies that fuel chronic stress. (see BOOTSTRAP Process)

Resistance – one of the two prime *stress intensifiers* addressed by the BOOTSTRAP system, *resistance* is the mental habit of going to war with the one thing that can be no different from how it is: this moment—or *what's on the screen. Resistance* is caused by a repetitive thought "this should not be like this." (see Week 2)

Restore – The third step in the three-step BOOTSTRAP system. *Restore* refers to the return of the body, mind, and nervous system to a natural, healthy state as a result of the *recognition* and *release* of unhelpful mental habits and tendencies. (see BOOTSTRAP Process)

Scientific Observation – One of the five BOOTSTRAP techniques involving a commitment to study the relationship between one's actions and their results as they pertain to the creation of stress. (see BOOTSTRAP Techniques)

Stress – A term first coined by Hungarian-born endocrinologist Hans Selye in 1936 to refer to the response of the body and mind to "any demand for change." Said another way, stress is the body's attempt to respond to a particular circumstance in a way that will best ensure its survival. (see Stress: Friend or Foe)

Stress Intensifiers – The mental habits that worsen the experience of stress. The BOOTSTRAP system directly addresses two prime stress intensifiers: *resistance* and *disintegration.* (see Week 2 & 3)

Stress Lab – The room or other place in the home where the daily BOOTSTRAP techniques are performed. (see BOOTSTRAP Overview)

Stress Response – The automatic response of the body and mind to a change in circumstance or perceived threat. Managed by the *sympathetic nervous system,* the *stress response* yields a state of heightened awareness and readiness that when allowed to persist over time, can overtax the body's resources. (see Stress: Friend or Foe)

Stress Trigger – Any event or situation that triggers the body's *flight-or-fight* or *stress response*. The trigger may be a change in circumstance, like a new job; or a legitimate threat, like a disease diagnosis; or it may simply be a situation, sound, image, smell, taste, or even thought that triggers memories of a threat. See also *threat*. (see BOOTSTRAP Overview and Stress: Friend or Foe)

Stressologist – A participant in the BOOTSTRAP system. The term refers to how BOOTSTRAP is designed to help users understand the workings of stress through experiential experimentation. Like any successful scientist, the most effective BOOTSTRAP participants bring a healthy dose of curiosity and dedication to the process. (see BOOTSTRAP Overview)

Suffering – Refers to the anxiety, frustration, conflict, and irritation that are added to the pain of an experience through resistance. Distinct from *pain*, *suffering* is a self-created phenomenon and thus is an optional part of an experience. See also *pain* and *resistance*. (see Week 2)

Sympathetic Nervous System – That portion of the nervous system responsible for preparing the body and mind to deal with threatening circumstances. When faced with a threat, real or perceived, the *sympathetic nervous system* releases stress hormones into the blood stream (epinephrine, norepinephrine, and cortisol primarily), which prompt the body and mind into a state of heightened readiness. See also *fight-or-flight response*. (see Stress: Friend or Foe)

Threat – A person or situation that is *perceived* as a *threat*. A perceived threat, whether it is real or imagined, triggers the body and mind's *stress response*. See also *stress trigger*. (see BOOTSTRAP Overview)

What's on the Screen – refers to what is happening in this very moment. Much like *what's on the screen* in a movie theater, the defining nature of *what's on the screen* in life, because it is already happening now, cannot be any different from how it is—at least in this moment. (see Week 1)

ABOUT THE AUTHOR

Eric Walrabenstein is nationally-recognized educator and speaker in the fields of yoga, mindfulness, and mind-body wellness. As a former infantry officer in the U.S. Army, he knows first-hand of the dedication and sacrifices the members of our armed forces make every day.

Since his separation from the service over two decades ago, Eric has devoted his life to mining the ancient wisdom of yoga, meditation, and mindfulness in order to translate their timeless secrets for artful and stress-free living in modern life.

In addition to his work with BOOTSTRAP, he is the founder of Yoga Pura, one of Arizona's largest yoga and wellness centers and is the president of BetterBox, a first-of-its-kind company specializing in the creation of customized personal-development experiences.

Learn more about Eric and his work at: www.EricWal.com

ABOUT BOOTSTRAP

BOOTSTRAP is a first-of-its-kind yoga system designed specifically to help heal military-related stress conditions, including post-traumatic stress.

The seven-week, curriculum-driven program combines yoga's science of mind with the latest modern stress-management principles and has been proven effective in less than one hour per day.

While originally conceived to help our troops and veterans, the program has wide-ranging relevance for anyone wanting to live more artfully and happily. BOOTSTRAP is designed to be performed in the privacy of one's own home and is available for military members and veterans free of charge.

Learn more at: www.bootstrapUSA.com